D0946442

LIBRARY

Gift of

The Bush
Foundation

Kenny Salwey's

TALES OF A
RIVER
RAT

Adventures along the Wild Mississippi

Voyageur Press

First published in 2005 by Voyageur Press, an imprint of MBI Publishing Company, Galtier Plaza, Suite 200, 380 Jackson Street, St. Paul, MN 55101-3885 USA.

Text copyright © 2005 by Kenny Salwey

All rights reserved. No part of this work may be reproduced or used in any form by any means—graphic, electronic, or mechanical, including photocopying, recording, taping, or any information storage and retrieval system—without written permission of the publisher.

Edited by Danielle J. Ibister
Designed by Julie Vermeer
Printed in the United States of America

Cover photograph reproduced by permission of Andrew Graham-Brown. Front flap illustration by Bob Hines and back cover illustration by Tom Kelley are courtesy of the U.S. Fish and Wildlife Service.

Library of Congress Cataloging-in-Publication Data

Salwey, Kenny, 1943-
  Kenny Salwey's tales of a river rat : adventures along the wild Mississippi.
    p. cm.
  ISBN 0-89658-649-9 (hardcover)
  1. Salwey, Kenny, 1943- 2. Salwey, Kenny, 1943- 3. Naturalists--Wisconsin--Biography. 4. Hunting--Mississippi River Region--Anecdotes. 5. Fishing--Mississippi River Region--Anecdotes. 6. River life--Mississippi River Region--Anecdotes. I. Title.
  QH31.S16A3 2005
  508.775'092--dc22

                    2005018834

MBI titles are also available at discounts in bulk quantity for industrial or sales-promotional use. For details write to Special Sales Manager at MBI Publishing, Galtier Plaza, Suite 200, 380 Jackson Street, St. Paul, MN 55101-3885 USA.

Page 1: Kenny spends a long day push-poling the river rat way. (Photograph © Mary Kay Salwey)

Page 3: Illustration by Tom Kelley, courtesy of the U.S. Fish and Wildlife Service

QH
31
.S16
A3
2005

042106-2515 D8

*T*his book is dedicated to my parents, Willard and Melvina Salwey. Both were born "hill country folk" close to the river where they have lived well over ninety years. They allowed me at a very early age to learn about and to love Nature.

Over the past sixty-two years, I have thought of them in a two-word phrase: Pappa and Momma, Pa and Ma, Mom and Dad, Mother and Father. However, "wonderful parents" says it best.

Kenny poses in the doorway of the Marsh Shack with his dog Spider. (Photograph © Carl Lacher)

CONTENTS

Rat Tales

Illustration by Tom Kelley, courtesy of the U.S. Fish and Wildlife Service

Foreword

by Andrew Graham-Brown

Andrew Graham-Brown is an independent producer and director specializing in wilderness filmmaking. He spent two years with Kenny Salwey in the Upper Mississippi River valley creating the wildlife documentary Mississippi: Tales of the Last River Rat. *Commissioned by the BBC and the Discovery Channel and produced through Andrew's production company @GB Films, the film won a Best Television Program award, as well as merit awards for conservation message and editing, at the Missoula International Wildlife Film Festival (2005). Andrew lives in Bristol, England.*

My fortune is my memory of distant people and far-off lands. As a filmmaker, I've ridden wild horses in Outer Mongolia and tracked black rhinos on the African plains with the San Bushmen—the oldest, and to my mind, most naturally resourceful people on earth. Recently, I ran away from the diabolical bloodcurdling intentions of a charging Komodo dragon—funny now, but not then. Once upon a time, I experienced (firsthand) the primeval joy of making fire the ancient way—two sticks rubbed together to make a spark—with the aboriginal people of Australia's Northern Territories. But the story I most like to brag about down the pub is the time I was in the core of the Big Apple. Out of the blue, I got a call from the BBC in England: "Andrew, would you mind interviewing Keith Richards tomorrow afternoon, roundabout teatime at his home in Connecticut, New England?" I was on a roll. Here was a case of being in the right place at the right time. The sliding doors opened, I stepped into the master's drawing room, and a living legend sung me the blues.

Today, I've got the blues. I'm sitting here at home in England on a depressingly drizzly day that so typifies my hometown of Bristol in March. I could let my mood be dampened, but instead I elevate my spirits by reflecting on my proudest and most treasured filmmaking experience: two years spent travelling the backwaters of the Upper Mississippi River with a man I've come to call my father.

My real dad lives in the Cotswolds, quintessential picture-postcard England. Along with my beloved mother, he nurtures a most beautiful garden. The organically toiled soil burgeons with life even in the dead of winter. My dad first met Kenny on the "veg patch" among the brussels sprouts in autumn. I know from their talk back and forth that my old man approves of me appropriating his title to speak of my

Overleaf: Kenny saunters streamside while visiting England to create the soundtrack of the documentary Mississippi: Tales of the Last River Rat. *(Photograph © Andrew Graham-Brown)*

sage-like friend, Kenny Salwey—a man renowned the world over for his poetic prose and elegantly simple philosophy of nature.

Through my eyes, the Mississippi and Kenny Salwey are one and the same. He is my first and last impression of the big river. We've walked and talked sense and nonsense on winter's thick mantle of ice; dug the pungent skunk cabbage root during the verdant joy of spring; wiled away the dog days of summer near cool streams, fishing for elusive brook trout; and we've sat together, content in silence, marvelling at the outstanding colours of fall.

Once on a fine summer's day, I sat in Kenny's canoe gabbling in a rather loud voice about nothing in particular and Kenny paused on his oar to say, "A June morning wouldn't be complete without the sound of birdsong. The birds all sing in a different key, they sing a different song, and they all sing at the same time. It makes a beautiful lullaby. It is salve to the soul. Yet, if us humans were to try and do that, we couldn't stand it in the same room."

"Life is too short to hurry through it," the old sage once told me during a lunch break on the riverbank. He'd seen me wolfing down his delightful ninety-two-year-old mother's delicious homemade apple pie. I was chomping at the bit, urging Kenny to break out of his "lazy old-man-river routine" and get his proverbial arse in gear. I thought of ditching his oars for a 100-horsepower engine, a petroleum-driven technology that could propel our canoe to the next location in time for "magic hour"—the fleeting moments of light at day's end that wildlife filmmakers crave to record to craft their version of exquisite nature. As I paddled the swift and steady current downstream, I thought about Kenny's wise words, ditched my watch, and took time to slow down and take pleasure in the natural world all around. I began to hear and see the gorgeous, integrally linked details bound together in the ancient rhythms of what Kenny calls the Circle of Life. The gurgling waters of the Mississippi that keep on going round and round, the whisper of cottonwood leaves, and the hover-dance of dragonflies above the water's surface. *Life is too short to hurry through it.* It is a simple yet profound statement, and Kenny reminded me during our times exploring the beauty of the seasons that "there is greatness in simplicity."

We first met at Big Lake Shack, known to some as the lair of the last Mississippi river rat. It stands a canoe-length square, a stone's throw from the water's edge. On the black tar-stained oak door, a bright yellow sign reads "La Maison de Salwey"—in homage, I later learn, to his French-Canadian roots. Our shaking of tentative hands was a bit like two inquisitive dogs meeting in the park for the first time. The city boy, armed head to toe with every conceivable survival gadget and gizmo known to modern man, meets swamp hermit, who some fools might reckon has spent too many years in the woods, holed up in a log cabin he built with his own hands and sweat. Kenny raised what we in England call "a very hairy eyebrow" and said many words in his singular utterance: "Uh-huh." All the same, "the old man of the woods" reassured me with a full-toothed smile and he graciously ushered me over the threshold of his shack into a world where I will always feel at home. It reminds me of my grandfather's potting shed at the end of his flower garden in an old part of England called the New Forest. The beguiling interior, chock-a-block with the paraphernalia and memorabilia of a life spent subsisting in the wild, says so much about the man. Where my grandfather hung dried flowers, Kenny hangs fishing lures, snapping turtle shells, and raccoon tails. Grandpa used a non-alphabetical filing cabinet of Clan tobacco tins to stash mementoes and letters from his harrowing teenage years in the trenches of World War I. Kenny, on the other hand, employs a trusty old Copenhagen snuff tin to store grubs he harvested from the galls of last year's goldenrod prairie plant—nature's gift of bait to catch sunfish and crappies.

Home is where the hearth is, and Kenny's shack, I soon found out, is the only place to be when the wind's howling twenty-five degrees below zero. Made cozy beside the wood-burning stove, I spent many nights transfixed by flame, in wonderment of the witty and insightful tales of life on the river, the old-timer's way. These stories were being told by a masterful storyteller in a voice "as soothing as stroking a cat," as a distinguished film critic from England would later comment. Kenny's voice is a musical instrument. While I listened, entranced by stories of beaver trapping and moonshine, I tried to picture a way of life that many lament for passing into a bygone era.

One day, out in the swamp, swarms of deerflies and mosquitoes gathered around me in a bloodsucking frenzy. Slathering myself in toxic chemicals that did nothing to assuage their hunger and everything to poison my body, I wondered why these flying battalions were not also bombarding the River Rat. "Hog lard dope," Kenny told me with a knowing twinkle in his eye. It is a natural and effective potion made from a secret recipe of roots and herbs, handed down through generations of rivermen.

Kenny Salwey is a keeper of the old ways. The stories he has scribed within the pages of this lovely book strike a fundamental cord within us all. They tell of a time when man belonged to nature and not the other way around. "When it rains," Kenny once told me in a Zen-like moment of metaphorical wisdom, "the President is going to get just as wet as I am."

Kenny canoes through swamp waters with his constant traveling companions, Spider and Webster, during the filming of Mississippi. *(Photograph © Andrew Graham-Brown)*

FOREWORD by Neil Rettig

Neil Rettig is an Emmy-winning natural history filmmaker and conservationist whose work has helped protect threatened ecosystems and endangered species around the world. In filming Mississippi: Tales of the Last River Rat, *he turned his cinematic eye toward the Big River and the life of Kenny Salwey. Neil has also worked for National Geographic, IMAX, and Disney, among others. He lives in the Mississippi River town of Prairie du Chien, Wisconsin.*

I grew up in northern Illinois, thirty miles from Chicago. Our home was next to a wild area that you could walk through for two miles without hitting a fence or a road. By the time I was fourteen, I kept a collection of snapping turtles, snakes, frogs, and salamanders. My parents encouraged my interest in nature. One summer, my mom signed me up for a correspondence course in taxidermy and tolerated the family freezer overflowing with "specimens."

Nature and filmmaking merged in my late teens when I picked up a film camera and never put it down. Since those early days, I've traveled the world, filming wildlife and wild places. In 1989, after a film assignment on the Mississippi River, I settled outside of Prairie du Chien, Wisconsin. My knowledge of the River, though, always just scratched the surface.

Today, I feel a new intimacy with the Mississippi. My eyes have opened wide, and I feel a rebirth of awareness.

My new understanding started the day I began reading *The Last River Rat* by Kenny Salwey and J. Scott Bestul. Kenny's picture on the cover sparked my curiosity, and the book took me on a voyage and celebration of the Upper Mississippi River, a look at the seasons, from the perspective of a rare and gifted man. I felt a powerful sense of kinship with Kenny's view of the natural world. To me, he was a hero, a legend in his time. I wanted to meet this legendary river rat.

Not only did I meet Kenny but we became warm friends while working on a BBC/Discovery film about the Upper Mississippi River as seen through Kenny's sensitive eyes. We worked together filming *Mississippi: Tales of the Last River Rat* for the better part of two years.

Those two years changed my life. Not only did I learn much from Kenny about the river, I also learned about myself—my weaknesses and my strengths. And I saw the natural world in a new, very bright light.

"The only thing constant on the river is change." Those words from Kenny really hit home. Change: it can take a million years or a split second. I paid careful attention to change all around me, in my life and on the river. I learned that Nature does not wait; it keeps moving along. I learned that procrastination can mean missed opportunities. "We can do it tomorrow"—but on the river, and in life, tomorrow it might rain. Sometimes, I learned the hard way. Events on the Mississippi often surface for a short time, then disappear, swallowed up by the currents of time. Capturing the events, those magic moments, meant "striking while the fire was hot."

In a place of such contrasting seasons, change is truly constant. A winter snowstorm, sheets of ice like plate glass moving along the river's surface. The peak of fall colors, turtle eggs hatching. Sunrise, sunsets—a flow of events, no time to waste in this vibrant and constantly changing world.

Even as he taught me to seize the moment, Kenny also taught me to slow down and appreciate life. "No need to rush; life's too short to hurry through." This is one of my favorites of Kenny's sayings. He is so right. When a person takes a walk in the woods, slowing down just a bit makes the difference in seeing or missing something special. This philosophy applies to everything as we travel through life. I think about the importance of slowing down when I remember working with Amerindians deep in the Amazon. They move fast to get from point A to point B, but while making observations, they move at the pace of the forest: slow and encompassing.

Kenny is a gifted writer. Those of us who love the outdoors soak up Kenny's words and are bathed in the essence of his metaphors. In the tale "Dusky and Red," Kenny takes the simple experience of befriending two squirrels, something most people would not even consider, and tells a deeper, more profound story. Kenny sends a powerful message at the end of this story and shows that man, even Kenny himself, can leave deep, damaging footprints in the forest. This story brings tears to my eyes. I relate to his experience with my own personal blunders with nature and living.

Kenny's most cherished gift to me is the inspiration he gives by just being himself. Just like his canoe gliding through the dark backwaters, Kenny's attitude always stays even keel. During the film production, we had some setbacks and technical problems, in particular with the sound. Kenny's patience amazed me; it always flowed in the same direction, toward the positive. As we progressed in production, I could see the story and images shaping up. Kenny's camera presence and professionalism motivated me to walk the extra mile, to sink my teeth into every sequence, to give everything I had to make it right. I felt encouraged to overcome many challenges during the filming and motivated to use my camera as an expression of my feelings and Kenny's insights into Nature's magic.

To me, the most astounding of Kenny's many attributes is his ability to speak from the heart, from his very soul. Not once in the field was anything scripted. You can look into those eyes filled with wisdom and sincerity and be sure he is speaking the truth.

In particular, I was moved by a sequence we did on duck hunting. After a successful hunt, we filmed Kenny sharing his views on the ethics of hunting. I have never been more moved by a man's insight. His words hit home with power and conviction:

When we build our shopping malls, our highways, our artificial world, and we take away the critter's homes, we take them away forever, not just for today. We don't just kill one duck today to eat; we kill ducks that would have survived, would have thrived, would have reproduced for generation after generation.

Kenny and I will remain good friends forever.

Water lotus float in the Upper Mississippi River National Wildlife and Fish Refuge. (Courtesy of the U.S. Fish and Wildlife Service)

Acknowledgments

I shall always remain indebted to my "family" at Voyageur Press, in particular Danielle Ibister, the editor of this book. She sorted through my longhand scribblings with much patience, kindness, and sound advice.

Thank you, Andrew Graham-Brown, my river rat "son" in Bristol, England, for your kind thoughts about the Big River and my "rat tales."

I consider Neil Rettig to be my friend and kindred spirit. We are both river rats. The only differences are the tools we use to make a living with Nature. Neil uses his creative eye and his camera in unequaled ways. Thank you, Neil, for your foreword.

A special thank you to my beloved Mary Kay for writing the introduction to this book as only you could. You know me better than anyone else in the world. You have faith in me and give me strength and encouragement when I need it most. Thank you, my dear.

For as long as the robin sings and the green grass grows with the coming of spring, I will be grateful to you, the reader, for showing an interest in the Big River and this old river rat's tales.

Kenny Salwey, the Last River Rat (Photograph © Andrew Graham-Brown)

Introduction

by Mary Kay Salwey

Ph.D., State Wildlife Education Specialist,
Wisconsin Department of Natural Resources

Some folks say that Kenny Salwey, the Last River Rat, cut his teeth on a canoe paddle and seasoned it with Mississippi mud. He's certainly the last of a breed of men whose lifestyle has all but disappeared in this fast-paced, high-tech world. Kenny Salwey is unconventional by every measure of the word. He has lived a hard life, a life harder than most of his readers could ever imagine. He grew up living, working, playing, and fighting—sometimes for his life—in the natural world. He grew to love that world of Nature and to shun the artificial world of his fellow human travelers, a world filled with TVs, cell phones, DVDs, satellite dishes, computers, and wristwatches. He earned a living with the land, close to Nature and the Mississippi River, all his life using only his native wit and intelligence.

This unconventional woodsman has made a meager but satisfying living through thirty years sharing Nature's bounties, getting by as a river guide, trapper, fisherman, hunter, root and herb collector, and all-round woodsman. Kenny thrives in the seasonal cycle of life, in rhythm with Nature. He gathers wild fall mushrooms and digs ginseng roots in September; hunts ducks, geese, grouse, and pheasant come

October; tracks the whitetail each November; and traps muskrat, mink, and beaver from December through April. Come spring, he hunts wild turkey and gathers wild morels. He fishes for trout in June and for pan fish under a leafy tree in the heat of summer.

Living amidst Nature for decades, Kenny has acquired a commanding knowledge of the area's plants and animals. Some say he's a bit of a "swamp witch" because he knows a number of age-old herbal remedies for what ails you. He's got special potions for poison ivy rashes, grayish goo for spider bites, and wild root teas for sore throats. He slathers up his shirt and hat with a yellow "fragrant" balm "gare-own-teed" to keep the mosquitoes away, as well as just about any other critter—beast or man—that might happen by.

Kenny's paternal ancestors can be traced back to the Alsace-Lorraine district on the border between France and Germany. They emigrated from there to Canada in the mid-1850s, settling in the area near Montreal, Quebec, where their bloodline, as the family stories go, was influenced by the Woodland Cree. The sense of Native American spirituality and reverence for the land is evident in Kenny's outlook on the natural world. His maternal ancestors hailed from Switzerland. All his great-grandparents eventually moved to Buffalo County, Wisconsin, where they—and his grandparents and parents—eked out a living on small subsistence farms.

Kenny was born July 12, 1943, in his mother's bed in the old farmhouse that once belonged to his pioneering grandparents in the heart of Wisconsin's rugged hill country, about four miles east of the Mississippi River. The farmstead is still there, close to a sleepy, curbless country community called Waumandee.

His mother reports that it was "hotter than blazes" that July day. Back then, country doctors still made house calls, so old Doc Meile came out from nearby Cochrane to deliver baby Kenny. Doc Meile made Kenny's mother stay in bed for two sweltering weeks. She still recounts those stifling days with a sense of happiness mixed with misery.

Most readers will find it a tad difficult to identify with the country lifestyle here in Buffalo County. Kenny's home-land of backwater sloughs, steep hills, and sheer bluffs in western Wisconsin is largely overlooked. In a way, the area is comparable to the Ozarks or Appalachia, minus the water. Not many people can survive the harsh realities of this rough and rugged country: sweeping springtime floods; soggy, mosquito, and black fly–infested swamps; slippery hillsides; steep, unplowed, icy winter roads; and poor soil that's either too sandy or too perpendicular to plow. A mile or less east of the River, everything is up, then down, then up again. This tough living may be one of the reasons Buffalo County residents live such long lives, many well into their nineties and even hundreds.

Buffalo County generally has been twenty years be-hind the times. Most of the old-time hotels, hardware stores, and grocery stores have folded up. There's only one stoplight in the entire county, and most folks think that's one too many. The people who grew up along the River or tucked high in the hills are quintessentially persistent folk—and strong, but sometimes as stubborn as an old wet mule. The biggest town has only 2,000 people; the total county population is 13,900. There are more cows than people here. Not surprisingly, many folks are related to each other. That makes them friendly as can be but also a wee bit clannish. They stick together in hard times but mostly to each other. They are suspicious of outsiders. In recent years, city-dwellers seeking to get away from hectic urban life have bought up woodland at prices the locals can't afford. Up goes another hunting shack or metal pole shed on the once pristine countryside, or another guest cottage hanging tenaciously from the hills, or another mansion on the bluff overlooking the Great River Road. The end result? The Great River Road ain't so great-looking anymore, the local landowner's taxes are driven up, and the farmers are driven out. While they claim deed to "their" land, these transplants rarely become part of the community. Seldom do they bond with the folks whose families toiled to make the first paths, the first roads, the first farmsteads in this rugged country. In addition, many of the forested hillsides for which outsiders pay outrageous prices have been logged prior to sale by wily local owners. Nevertheless, these urbanites are the first ones to sign up for woodland tax relief. They can afford a second home but apparently they can't afford to pay the taxes. It is common in Buffalo County to find comparable lands, located next to each other, one with taxes in the thousands and the other with taxes in the hundreds. Who is really supporting the community?

In the days when Kenny was growing up, every little river town along the Mississippi had a half-dozen or so hardworking families who made a living along the River by gill netting, seining, digging ginseng, trapping, and hunting. They called it living off the land. But to Kenny, living "off" the land is living like a parasite, a bloodsucker, a louse, a wood tick. He prefers the notion that he lives with the land, in harmony with it, not separate or above it.

When the Great Depression hit Buffalo County, the families still ate mighty fine. There were no soup lines in town. For certain, life was tough, but these folks survived by eating the meat they hunted each fall and the fish they caught with hook and line each summer. They supplemented these activities by growing vegetable gardens and raising a few hogs and chickens.

Kenny grew up in the post–World War II era when most of the nation's farms had been modernized. Even so, many of Buffalo County's isolated farmers still tenaciously worked their land with their horses well into the 1950s. But modern agriculture practices finally caught up with them, too. Along with tractors and combines came DDT, the powerful, now banned, pesticide. Kenny's father used this poison, mixing it up in an old milk can. After adding the powder and water, he'd stir it with his bare arm. Chemical companies, extension agents, and soil conservationists told everybody it was safe.

They sprayed it everywhere—and it worked terrifically on pests, so the farmers kept on using it.

Pretty soon, however, the bald eagle population plummeted. Whippoorwills, meadowlarks, and bobwhite took it on the chin, too. When Kenny was young, the whippoorwills called in the meadows at night outside his window as he'd drift to sleep. Each morning, the meadowlarks and quail would sing on the wooden fence posts, especially after a rainstorm. Bluebirds nested in the cavities of rotting fence posts. Kenny has witnessed the decline of these meadowland birds, which rely on the insects in farm fields and meadows. DDT essentially eliminated their food supply.

On top of that, expansions in farming cut into these birds' habitats. To stay solvent, farmers kept making their fields larger, increasingly turning to cash crops rather than the more labor-intensive beef or dairy herds, and they shunned traditional farming methods. Fewer cows and horses on the farm meant the pastures and back meadows could be worked for a profit. Grassland birds, being ground nesters, were prone to predation by the increasing population of farm-dwelling predators such as opossums, skunks, raccoons, and feral barn cats. Kenny believes that intensive farming—with its combination of habitat loss, increased predation, and increased use of pesticides—is the main culprit in the decline of these meadowland creatures.

Despite the current bans on DDT and some other nasty farm pesticides, spraying poisons on our crops is still the norm. Kenny laments that we don't know what all these chemicals are doing to people, to critters, or to the land. "The ag-chemical industry comes out with new stuff all the time, saying 'This is safe for use. This is okay now.' Well, how do they know it's safe? We're lucky if they do a six-month study," Kenny grieves. "More often than not, the more important long-term research is lacking. Now we've got all those chemicals in the Mississippi watershed, draining into the tributaries and eventually into the River itself. The chemicals are probably contaminating our drinking water, too, particularly in those areas along the river where the soil is so sandy that the poisons can percolate down into the water table in no time at all."

Another bird that has taken a beating in this area—especially in the hill country where trout streams run fresh and clear across the valley floor—is the "shy-poke," or great blue heron. "You know, it isn't unusual for a farmer to take his rifle out and blow one down," Kenny says. "It happens. It's just a fact of life. Even today, friends of mine apparently still don't understand and appreciate the role these creatures play in Nature and would rather shoot them than marvel at their wonderful adaptations. We have to begin to learn that what's good for the land and what's good for the critters is good for the people. If it ain't good for the land or for the critters, it ain't gonna be good for the people."

Kenny's small hill-country farm sat close to a little stream that fed the Waumandee Crick. Periodically, Kenny and his family ventured down the steep country roads, known locally as "dugways," to the Mississippi River. They'd fish, spear carp, trap, and do other river-related activities. So while he was born in the hill country, he became a river rat at an early age. He grew up carefree. He came and went the way he wanted. He had no fear of the woods or the creeks. To him, these were good places. He loved to crawl up in the hills and pretend he was an eagle or a red-tailed hawk. From atop the bluffs, he could see everything. He spent his youth, in his words, "attending to fishin', huntin', and trappin' more so than to readin', writin', and 'rithmatic."

In his sixth summer, after the wobbly legs of toddler-hood had stabilized and his mother could trust him to be on the farm alone, he learned to trap pocket gophers. He was so little and scrawny that he had to stand on a Victor #1 gopher trap spring just to set it. Pocket gophers were the scourge of farmers. Gophers create mounds of dirt as they excavate the topsoil. Many times, hay mowers or grain binders struck these mounds and were damaged; therefore, a twenty-five-cent bounty was paid for each gopher trapped. Kenny would take his catch down the road about a mile to Ole and Sally's Tavern and sell the "varmints." Then he'd take his credit in trade for some valuables: a bottle of soda pop, some Bazooka bubble gum, or a Fudgesicle.

That September, Kenny experienced one of the most traumatic—as he tells it—experiences of his life: His mother told him he had to go to school. Elementary school for Kenny was a little, wooden, one-room schoolhouse that sat in a small grove of trees one-half mile from the family farm. He spent his first year just trying to write his name.

He marvels at how today kids that age can usually read and spell just about everything. It never got any better for him. He didn't take to school. He would have rather looked out the window and dreamt of hunting in the hills or fishing in the creek. He would have just as soon chewed the covers off his books than read them. He rarely missed an opportunity to play hooky.

When Kenny was eight years old, if his father didn't need his help with farm chores, he'd sneak out back to explore a deep, unpastured gully. He and his brother eventually built a little wooden shack in that hundred-foot eroded gash in the earth. He asked his mother for an old cast-iron frying pan and his father for the BB gun. Since the creek wasn't far from his shack, he'd carry down an old cane pole, wrap a couple of fishhooks in a piece of tape, and pocket a sinker or two and an old rusty jackknife. He'd also carry his lucky copper penny and a special "magic rock" in his pants pockets. In his little wilderness kingdom, he'd wile away his boyhood free time exploring, hunting, fishing, and gaining the first experiences he needed to become a self-sufficient backwoodsman. This was his special place—and the biggest wilderness in the world to him. In little-boy terms, it was huge; in reality, it was only several acres.

Eventually, young Kenny made it to high school. He began at the old Cochrane High. It was small, about ninety-six students all told. Then, the parents of the area decided to save money and consolidate the country schools into one great big school district. They closed all the one-room

RIVER RAT COUNTRY

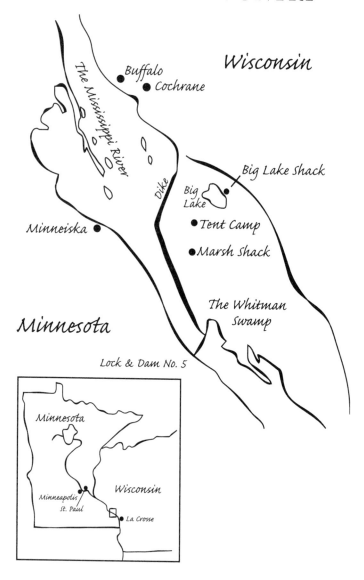

Wisconsin

The Mississippi River

• Buffalo
  • Cochrane

Dike

Big Lake Shack •

Big Lake

• Tent Camp

• Marsh Shack

Minneiska •

The Whitman Swamp

Minnesota

Lock & Dam No. 5

Minnesota

Wisconsin

Minneapolis
St. Paul

• La Crosse

schoolhouses, believing "bigger is better," and the Co-chrane–Fountain City School District was created. All three levels—elementary, junior high, and high school—were connected on the same sprawling campus. Kids no longer walked to school; they were bussed (now that's a real savings, isn't it?).

Today, tobacco, drug, and alcohol abuse plague the huge school system. Kids can't even bring a pocketknife through the front door. Back when the community was involved, when everyone knew everyone else, a teacher never worried about what a kid carried in his pockets—unless, of course, it was a toad or snake—because a kid would never dream of using his pocketknife on anyone at school. It was unheard of and such a thought never occurred. Pocketknives were tools used for whittling, cutting fishing line, cleaning trout, and skinning squirrels and rabbits. A boy back then felt naked without his trusty old pocketknife. So, in certain ways, Kenny laments the modern school system.

Kenny somehow made it to graduation, but, having had it with farm chores, he decided that he knew more than his parents and certainly more than his teachers. He joined the U.S. Army and found himself in a most foreign land: New Jersey. He had never seen so many people in one place at one time. And, of course, it was an eye-opener to see people of different colors, different races, different nationalities, different regional dialects, and even different sexual orientations.

While Kenny was in the Army, his unit was selected for Special Forces training. This assignment landed him at Fort

Lewis in Washington state. During that time, he learned many survival skills. He was trained in the Olympic National Forest as a stealth soldier—the type of military man who can be dropped into any wilderness with minimal gear and survive until he completes his assignment.

When he was honorably discharged from the Army in 1962, Kenny's "career choices" were limited. He realized he'd missed out on something important in life, something precious called an education. Out there in the big bad world, he was at a disadvantage compared to those who had paid attention in school. So he played catch-up.

Kenny settled back into life along the River and began to see the value of books. He began to read. He read every book he could lay his hands on. He started guiding folks on the river. At the end of the day, they'd ask, "What do we owe you?" Kenny would reply, "Just send me a good book." Reading was, and still is, his hobby. He considers books some of the most precious things on Earth. "They can teach so much," he says. "The reader taps into someone else's brain, heart, and soul. Books can take you anywhere in the world, open up new horizons. And they do your brain good. When you read, you have to think. It's quite different from watching TV. I have a total disinterest in television. When most of the rest of American homes had TV sets, my family went without. It wasn't until I was in high school that my parents got their first set. I didn't watch it much back then and I don't watch it now. In fact, I couldn't even operate one of those darned push-button remote controls if my life depended on it!" He spent his nights in the swamp reading by a kerosene lamp. Today, he continues to read avariciously, mostly at bedtime in the winter. In the summer, he's generally out until dark; when he comes in, he's ready for bed.

Kenny's bookshelves are filled with the works of Ernest Thompson Seton, Henry David Thoreau, John Muir, Sigurd F. Olson, and Aldo Leopold. When I first met him, I thought I was witness to a miraculous reincarnation of the combined spirit of all these influential and powerful nature philosophers.

Kenny has read all of Thoreau's works. The first was *Walden*. He found a kindred spirit, even though Thoreau lived like Kenny for only two years. Thoreau's concept of greatness in simplicity caught Kenny's imagination. "Our world is far too complicated nowadays," Kenny says. "Our approach to the natural world is sometimes tainted by complexity, where it finally gets to looking so big, with so many people, that we sometimes throw our hands up and say, 'It's too much!' But if we look at it one day at a time and one step at a time, there is a timeless, unhurried rhythm there, a flow. Nature never hurries; the Circle of Life turns very slowly but very surely."

Aldo Leopold, author of *A Sand County Almanac*, also influenced Kenny's thinking. To him, Leopold's greatest gift was that he was an educated man—a college professor—yet his writing is simple, descriptive, and eloquent. He doesn't use Latin terms or fifty-cent words. Same with Sigurd Olson. Same with John Muir.

Reading about John Muir validated Kenny's experience. Muir had quit college to study in the greatest university in the world: the Outdoors. "Muir talked often about the tremendous therapeutic value of Nature," says Kenny. "It is no secret that Nature has wonderful therapeutic values that we cannot fully appreciate. I don't believe we can exist with any degree of happiness, or with a feeling of wellness and completeness, without Nature as a close part of our lives. It's still essential that we maintain some connection." Muir detested cities, calling them "concrete canyons," a name Kenny finds apt: "Laws that govern our behavior, actions, and attitudes toward Nature are made by people living in concrete canyons. I often thought that if politicians and natural resource agency officials had to decide on an issue in January, up to their butts in a snow bank, standing at the spot their decision is affecting, they'd make much wiser and more prudent decisions."

Kenny particularly likes that Muir found energy in Nature, and he loves the story about how Muir crawled up the highest tree he could find during a thunderstorm. "Some might say he didn't quite have both oars in the water, but you know, many people ahead of their times are often thought of as eccentric," Kenny says. "Time generally proves just how foresighted they really were. And that's the shame of it. Most of them were not accepted in their own lifetimes. Sigurd Olson generally was, and Leopold was, too, but not to the degree they are renowned today. Thoreau certainly wasn't. He was thought of as a real oddball. Someone asked

Thoreau once, 'Why don't you take more trips?' He took one trip to the Mississippi, one to Maine, and he floated the Merrimack River with his brother one time. But he replied, 'Why should I go elsewhere when I'll never learn all there is to know about Concord, Massachusetts?' I feel that way myself. I think that slogan 'Think globally, act locally' is right on. Most of us aren't ever going to go to the rain forest. So let's take care of our backyards first. Certainly let's be concerned about the rain forest, be aware of its plight and support efforts there. But let's focus on our own backyards first, and we will make a difference.

"Another thing about Muir was his ideas about preservation, preserving the great forests and parks. This was way back, before there was a real need in America to preserve such places. He could see down the road a ways. That's something we all need to consider. We need to think seven generations ahead. That's a Native American belief. Thinking only of what will be best for our children isn't thinking far enough ahead. We've got to think much farther than that."

Native American beliefs have also influenced Kenny. He likes to repeat a saying of Sitting Bull's. When the U.S. Army defeated the Lakota Sioux and forced the tribal members onto a reservation, the Sioux cried and lamented. Their way of life had come to an end. They would no longer roam the plains as nomads. The buffalo were gone and the one-time hunters had to live on a desolate reservation, relying on white man's handouts. The day they left for the reservation, the Sioux turned to Sitting Bull for advice. "What shall we do?" they asked. "How are we ever going to live?" He said, "As you follow your new path in life, what you come upon, pick it up. Examine it. Turn it over in your hands. Try it. If it doesn't suit you, drop it like you would a hot rock." Kenny has lived much of his life by that philosophy as he has negotiated the space between river rat and "civilized" man. Some things, like microwave ovens, he keeps. Other things, like the computer, he has tried, turning it over in his mind for awhile, but he didn't like the feel of it, so he dropped it like a hot rock. He decided to remain computer illiterate.

While Kenny busied himself at night playing catch-up, he made a living during the day doing things he had learned back home: trapping, hunting, fishing, digging roots, and collecting herbs for sale. So began his Swamp Odyssey. In his early backwoodsman's years, Kenny operated apart from mainstream America. He spent the biggest share of that life in one of the largest swamps and floodplain forests along the Upper Mississippi River. His stomping grounds consisted of about six thousand acres of seasonally flooded hardwood swamps and a few heavily forested sandy upland acres.

Floodplain forests are a rarity these days. They've steadily dwindled due to changes wrought by people. Twenty-nine locks and dams have been installed since the mid-1930s along the Upper Mississippi, from St. Louis, Missouri, to St. Paul, Minnesota. Once they were operational, the River was no longer natural. It became a series of reservoirs. Some of the floodplain forests didn't flood anymore; others became permanently flooded. The dams altered these wild places forever. The U.S. Army Corps of Engineers built so many dams and levees that the channeled River turned into nothing more than a great big barge canal.

The levee built to service the lock-and-dam section of Kenny's swamp is one of the longest dikes on the Upper Mississippi River. It extends over four miles long and it inadvertently created an area behind it free of river water. In the past twenty years, the Army Corps of Engineers has installed two sets of culverts in the dike that allow river water to enter the swamp. But the incoming muddy waters don't sprawl into the swamp; they remain inside the former slough banks. Because the bulk of Kenny's swamp is spring-fed, it contains some of the cleanest water anywhere. It also has a lot of aquatic vegetation, unlike the main channel. The River has lost much of its natural vegetation, mainly due to sedimentation and siltation from farming and other land-use practices along its tributaries.

The swamp, as remote and wild as it is, is far from quiet. The Upper Mississippi River valley is one of the largest and busiest river channels in America. Except on the windiest days, train whistles and tire whines penetrate deep into the swamp from train tracks and state highways on both sides of the channel. Groups that have visited Kenny there often complain about the incredible, constant noise.

Nevertheless, Kenny chose to live and work in the swamp. He eventually built three shacks there. Each was devoid of electricity, running water, or insulation. The outermost wooden Marsh Shack floats on barrels during high water. It's located about in the middle of the swamp. Kenny's most recent addition is Big Lake Shack, which sits on the eastern shore of the swamp. He coated its oak plank siding in old engine oil. Between the two shacks once floated the Tent Camp, made of canvas hung over peeled poles, which Kenny dismantled a number of years ago.

A trapper by trade, Kenny learned to observe animals and weather conditions or face the prospect of death in the wild. He immersed himself in the animals' environment. No track or natural disturbance went unnoticed. He learned how an animal would naturally act, where it would place its next footstep, why it was there, and where it would be tomorrow. He paid attention to weather patterns, moon phases, natural cycles—all the pieces of Nature's puzzle.

Even as careful and observant as he has been, Kenny still has faced a number of near-death experiences. He once waited out a blizzard, overnight, inside a hollow log, with only his dog for warmth. Surprisingly, for as much time as he spends around water, Kenny cannot swim well. The River, with its dangerous undertows and swift currents, has claimed many lives. Some were Kenny's friends. Once, on a riverbank outing with family and friends, Kenny was going down for the third time when a buddy rescued him; it's a story his mother recounts with fright in her voice. On several occasions while trapping, Kenny has fallen through the ice and entered the early stages of hypothermia. Not too many years ago, he was gored and trampled by a mean-spirited steer that had escaped through a local farmer's gate and entered the swamp (you can read about this adventure in more detail in the tale "Cowboy Kenny and the Swamp Steers"). Most recently, a deadfall crashed on his head as he was cutting firewood and knocked him unconscious. Miraculously, he has always avoided that final step toward death. However, these experiences have left him with a sense of insignificance in the great Circle of Life. He realizes what a little bitty speck he is—and we all are—"out there."

Not only did Kenny learn through reading and observing the natural world, he also learned through a sense of curiosity. He has always wanted to know how something happens. Why does it happen? Will it happen again? And he has an incredible ability to recall information. A person can learn all kinds of things but if the brain isn't trained to remember, the knowledge isn't worth much. Kenny learns things slowly, a piece at a time, but then he tucks that information away and builds on it. He finds this style of learning makes it easier to retain important information over a long period of time.

The people who have influenced Kenny are many and varied. Under the guidance of his father and other relatives, Kenny has constantly honed his keen observations of the natural world. Kenny's father was an influential figure in his early years. He was a busy, hard-working farmer but he always took a few moments during the course of the day to teach Kenny some ways of the wild. One spring morning, his father was in the woods splitting black oak logs for fence posts. He was about to cut down a tree but stopped and called Kenny to quick come see what he had just found. He pointed to a camouflaged nest containing nearly a dozen small partridge eggs.

Kenny and his father routinely hauled cow manure to the fields on a flatbed oak sled. It had sled runners and was pulled by a team of horses. They'd go up the hillside fields and throw off the natural fertilizer by hand. Many times before they'd start out, his father would grab the single-shot .22 rifle. When they'd get done with their chore, they'd tie the horses to a tree at the field's edge and wander into the hilly woods to hunt a squirrel or two for supper. Back then, local families never dreamed of taking hunting trips to far-off places. They had their own hunting grounds on their back forty.

Kenny's father, like most fathers at the time, believed that to spare the rod was to spoil the child. A "lickin'" was a common disciplinary action used in Kenny's youth. Kenny claims it hurt his pride more than his backside. Fathers back then often took old leather razor strops, used to sharpen straight-edged shaving razors, to the bottoms of their unruly children. Kenny's father hung his razor strop by the kitchen table. When Kenny or his brother fooled around once too often, his father tapped his butter knife on the table and looked at that razor strop. There wasn't a word said; it got real quiet around the table.

Kenny's maternal grandparents also had a big influence on him. Much of Buffalo County during his grandparents' youth consisted of enclaves of European immigrants. Different valleys contained different ethnic groups from Scandinavia, Germany, France, Ireland, or Poland. The folks in each valley spoke their homeland tongue, even in school. In Kenny's hometown of Waumandee, most residents spoke German or Polish at home. Kenny still vividly recalls his grandparents' thick German accent.

His grandmother had the most influence on him. She lived next door to the farm in a new house that Kenny's grandfather had built when Kenny's parents took over the farm after the Great Depression. His grandmother was calm and easygoing. She wore long flowing dresses covered with large aprons sporting huge pockets that sometimes contained cookies for Kenny. Grandma had a great big heart. She always had plenty of time to sit on her front porch and talk awhile. She was the best storyteller in the whole clan, and she lived to be ninety-eight years old. She loved campfires, listening to tree frogs forecast the rain, and gardening. It could be the hottest, most miserable weather—where a person sweats just sitting—with bugs being pesky around the farm, but Kenny's grandmother always looked at peace. She had a positive outlook and rarely complained. Kenny takes after her in that regard.

Kenny's grandmother used to tell him that everybody is given at least one special gift. Some never find it. In them, it just lies dormant. She'd often tell Kenny, "If you have a gift and uncover it, use it." Kenny realized he had the gift of storytelling, like his grandmother, but he took awhile to feel comfortable sharing his talents with others. He was a natural writer, too. He carried a pencil stub and an old calendar page folded in his pocket. Whenever he had a great thought, he'd stop and jot it down. He wrote poems, stories, and songs. He stored the scraps of paper in boxes—and never shared them with anybody.

Kenny tagged along with his grandmother in the hills when she picked blackberries. She wore her long dresses even in the woods and a big straw hat to keep the sun off. Women in those days didn't wear slacks or jeans. When she went berry picking, she wore a leather belt with a berry pail dangling from it. And she carried a stick to ward off rattlesnakes. The poisonous, and now endangered, timber rattlesnake used to be common in the Buffalo County hill country.

Most backwoods folks thought "the only good snake is a dead snake." That mindset is still common among the older folks but it is changing for the positive in youngsters' minds. Buffalo County, with its many unreachable and undeveloped craggy rock outcrops, harbors one of the last best places in the state to find snakes. Although Kenny grew up hunting rattlesnakes, today he believes there is no reason to kill any snake, even a rattlesnake. When encountered in the wild, a snake is probably more anxious to retreat from you than you are to retreat from it. Kenny never believed in killing any animal just to see it die. Each has its unique role to play in the Great Circle of Life. He respects all life—except maybe wood ticks.

Growing up, Kenny hung around older folks, the kind of people who had "been there–done that." He'd glean as much from them as he could, listening and watching more than talking. Two influential elders in Kenny's youth were his "uncles," Wilmer and Ed Salwey. Their dad and Kenny's grandfather were brothers. Kenny referred to Wilmer as "Uncle Whimpy." He was quite a character, a longtime river rat who loved milkshakes and trout fishing. Back then, the few surviving river rats were a secretive bunch. They rarely shared their knowledge with anyone wet behind the ears, because they had to survive themselves. Telling trade secrets was not the norm. However, Ed and Whimpy gladly took Kenny on their outings, whether they were trapping, ginseng digging, or rattlesnake hunting. Years ago, menfolk hunted rattlesnakes for bounty. Kenny tagged along with Uncle Whimpy on hot, humid summertime hunts. He still has a two-headed rattlesnake baby that he found inside a snake Uncle Whimpy killed when Kenny was ten years old. Kenny recalls the time a rattlesnake struck Uncle Whimpy on the forearm. The snake evidently had bit something the day before and used up its stock of venom because Whimpy never got very sick from it. Still, Whimpy's arm swelled up like a stovepipe and turned black and blue, and eventually the skin peeled off.

Snakes like to sun themselves on flat rocks in the summer. Rattlesnakes often den on the southeast point of a rocky bluff, where they can catch the morning and afternoon sun. Local folks call these open areas on the bluff tops "goat

*Illustration by Bob Savannah, courtesy of
the U.S. Fish and Wildlife Service*

prairies," because only a goat could climb the steep rocky
outcrops. Years ago, Buffalo County farmers burned the
prairies every spring, to keep the land open for pasturing
cattle. The only kind of tree that withstood the fire was the
bur oak. The fires were good for rattlesnakes, because it kept
their bluff tops open and sunny.

Farmers don't pasture their cattle as much these days, so
many goat prairies have grown into forested hillsides. The
resulting shade has eliminated the snakes' sunning spots,
which, even more than bounty hunting, has caused a decline
in the number of snakes. "We're losing more than the timber

rattlesnakes," Kenny muses. "We're losing the wildflowers as well. It's all about habitat loss. The only answer is to burn the goat prairies in the spring."

Kenny laments that the poisonous massasauga, or "swamp rattler," has gone the same route as the timber rattler. In his lifetime he has only found three massasaugas in the swamps, yet he's spent a good deal of time in their prime habitat. They like the flooded hardwood forest. The problem is only a few places remain where seasonally flooded hardwood forest occurs. Drainage ditches, dikes, expanding agriculture, tree-cutting, and bulldozing have all taken their toll. The Tiffany Bottoms State Wildlife Area along the Chippewa River is probably the last stronghold of this endangered rattlesnake in Buffalo County.

Kenny has always had different ideas and different ways of looking at things than most people. In his early adult years he lived a lifestyle that could be classified as hermit-like. He lived alone in the swamp in his lantern-lit shacks, subsisting on wild game, fish, and smoked jerky. He heated his shacks with the dead oaks he cut from his surroundings. He stayed away from people as much as he could. He was trying to prove something to himself and everybody else: that he could maintain a free and self-sufficient existence. In order to maintain that lifestyle, he took more than would be considered ethical—or legal—which explains why he has known every DNR warden in Buffalo County . . . personally. He has received his fair share of game citations. In those early years, he wanted nothing more than to hide in the swamp and hoard everything: the wild game, the secret places of the wild roots and herbs, all his experiences.

But as the years wore on, this man of the marsh realized he could no longer hoard his secret world of the Mississippi backwaters and bluffs. He could no longer maintain his solitary existence. Nature had done plenty for him; it had given him his life. He found that he just couldn't ask any more from Nature. Rather, he started asking himself, "What can I do for Nature?" He wanted to make a difference in people's lives, on behalf of Nature. He wanted to help make people's attitudes, values, ethics, and behaviors toward Nature more positive and respectful. That's what's most important to him these days.

He realized he had to reach, to teach, and to preach. Having grown more confident and full of conviction, he has taken his abundant experiences, personal stories, and deep-seated love for Nature on the road. He has become one of the most requested Nature speakers throughout the river valleys of Wisconsin, Minnesota, and Iowa. He talks about his self-sufficient life and the ecology of the Upper Mississippi River.

Kenny talks constantly about the natural world to anyone who will listen—to school children, troubled adolescents, church groups, and professional organizations such as the Wisconsin and Minnesota departments of natural resources. He speaks slowly, softly, and straight from the heart. He provokes, challenges, and sometimes incites his audience into a sense of action. Only two or three times has he heard negative comments from members of the hundreds of audiences he has entertained and educated. He delights in telling how one participant at a particularly serious and scientific water-quality conference described him as an "environmental wacko." One radio producer, before he got to know Kenny personally, worried about having him on the airwaves because he was "a bit on the fringe." Hopefully you won't perceive him as such but will look beyond his rough exterior, give second thought to his provocations, and seek the light which shines from his heart.

Kenny is unique among environmental educators. He is not the typical naturalist who helps visitors check off bird names or wildflowers on a list or who spouts an incredible array of natural history facts. He's unique because he speaks from his heart about Nature. The messages he relays may be subjective, but he definitely reaches a listener's "affective" side (their feelings) versus their "cognitive" side (their knowledge).

Through the time-honored art of storytelling, Kenny evokes scenes of life along the Big River, based on his true-life adventures in the swamps and backwoods. When asked whether his stories are "really true," he likes to quote Mark Twain: "for the most part." Kenny's nature talks, "rat tales," and unquenchable love for the River have inspired and educated people from all walks of life.

Kenny's outdoor education activities with K-12 classes began in the 1980s. He has garnered considerable attention and praise in the media. His lifestyle and educational programs have been featured on such television shows as *Wisconsin Magazine, Discover Wisconsin*, the *Dave Carlson Show, Northland Adventures*, Wisconsin Public Television's *Mississippi Stories*, Ron Schara's *Minnesota Bound*, and the *MacNeil-Lehrer News Hour*. Articles about Kenny, his philosophy, and his livelihood have appeared in *Wisconsin Trails* magazine, the *Milwaukee Journal Sentinel*, the *Isthmus* (Madison, Wisconsin), the *LaCrosse Tribune*, the *Journal Times* (Racine, Wisconsin), the *Pioneer Press* (St. Paul, Minnesota), and a host of other Midwest newspapers. Two books have featured chapters about his life, and he recently coauthored, with J. Scott Bestul, his first book, *The Last River Rat: Kenny Salwey's Life in the Wild*, which portrays a year of his life in the Mississippi backwaters.

In 1993, the Wisconsin Department of Natural Resources awarded Kenny its Western District's Educator of the Year Award. The award recognized Kenny as a leader in educating the people of Wisconsin about the natural values of the Mississippi River and its backwaters. In that year alone, he addressed more than four thousand people—ranging from five to one hundred years old—in Iowa, Minnesota, and Wisconsin. The award also acknowledged Kenny's development of a program called "A Holistic Approach to Environmental Education," which garnered grant support from the Wisconsin Environmental Education Board. The program allowed Kenny to take school teachers, 4-H leaders, and scout counselors into the area's swamps and bluff lands so they could gain an appreciation for these valuable natural resources.

In 2005, the mayor of Alma, Wisconsin, bestowed Kenny with a key to the city. The mayor proclaimed March 6, in honor of Kenny Salwey, "be designated as 'The Last River Rat Day' and that all respect and honor due a person of his renown be observed." This honor was bestowed upon him for the regional and national attention that *The Last River Rat* brought to his life and to the Upper Mississippi River region, as well as the international acclaim that the BBC/Discovery Channel–sponsored documentary *Mississippi: Tales of the Last River Rat* (produced by Andrew Graham-Brown/@GB Films of Bristol, England, and photographed by world-renowned wildlife and nature cinematographer Neil Rettig) gave to the River's backwaters, bluffs, swamps, and their ecosystems. It was also bestowed for Kenny's "tremendous accomplishment and many contributions he has made to society and to the Big River and to those who travel by canoe up and down it," in the mayor's words, and for Kenny's persistent championing of the environment.

I met this man a decade ago. He invited me to his shack, poled me through his swamp, and shared a campfire with me. I knew then that this man was a remarkable and unforgettable human being, a kindred spirit to me and to our beloved natural world. We couldn't have come from two more foreign backgrounds. But the glue of Nature bonded us together so tightly that we have become inseparable. Today, we labor ceaselessly in partnership for the betterment of our environment. Through his writings, I think you will come to know and love this man's reverence for the one world that supports us all. And, hopefully, you will be moved to become more involved in protecting the precious natural resources in your own little part of the universe.

Rat Tales

Illustration by Charles Douglas, courtesy of the
Canadian Museum of Nature

The Spring That Runs Forever

It was a hot, humid Sunday afternoon back in July 1959. My future wife, Faye, went inside to help her mother prepare supper while I joined the rest of her family in back of the little red house. A small group—Faye's father, brother, grandmother, and uncle—drank cold beer and chatted under the old elm and box elder trees.

"Hi Kenny," the uncle said, sticking out his hand and grinning. "My name's Johnny."

We shook hands, and I took a seat next to Grandma Sommers. The group resumed its conversation. I sized up Johnny, as was my habit. He was a small man, perhaps five foot seven or eight. His build was solid and stocky. He weighed maybe 185 or 190 pounds. His clothes were made of khaki, the long-sleeved shirt open a couple buttons at the top. His shoes were black string loafers. I noticed he addressed my future father-in-law as "Brother Bill." He wasn't talkative, but he had a firm handshake and was quick to laugh—good attributes of which I took note.

"Have any luck this morning?" Bill asked.

Johnny grinned. "Yah, I got a few, they're in the little Scotch cooler over there," he said, pointing toward the back of the house.

Johnny got up, walked over to the cooler, and brought it back to us. Carefully, he laid out eight of the most beautiful

German brown trout I'd ever seen. Their sleek, silvery brown bodies were flecked with red and yellow spots and tipped with white fins. Against the background of dark green grass, they looked spectacular. My eyes bugged out, my mouth fell slack, and my heart jumped a beat. It wasn't the size that boggled my mind. The largest was maybe sixteen inches, the smallest about eleven. It was their beauty, their magnificence, that captivated me.

I had cut my trout-fishing "eyeteeth" in the slow-moving, clay-bottom streams of west-central Wisconsin. The brown trout from those waters looked like streamlined carp. I would not have thought the trout of my boyhood fishing days and those lying at my feet were of the same species.

When I recovered my composure, I asked Johnny where he'd gotten them.

"Oh, over across the river," Johnny replied.

Across the river meant southeastern Minnesota, across the Mississippi from where we were in western Wisconsin. Johnny, who had never married, lived over there with Grandma Sommers, in the river city of Winona. I should have expected a vague answer to such a stupid question, knowing how secretive trout fishermen are about their favorite cricks. I dropped the subject.

Grandma Sommers told me how she sprinkles salt and lemon juice over the trout, puts a slice of onion in the head, wraps them in a damp cloth, and puts them on ice for twenty-four hours before frying them. It sounded mouthwatering good and only made me admire those fish more.

Later that afternoon, I overheard Bill and Johnny talking quietly. I caught parts of phrases like "Sandstone Hole . . . Willow Tree Hole . . . the old mill foundation still there . . . that big one still living in the second log hole in the woods?" My curiosity was whetted, to say the least!

Over the next several years, I saw Johnny occasionally at Brother Bill's house or at a family gathering. Our conversation usually turned to trout fishing, but Johnny never disclosed any specific cricks or tricks-of-the-trade. In my mind's eye, I never forgot those sparkling beauties lying in the summer grass.

The time was April 1963. It was one of those early spring days when, for the first time since winter, the air felt warm and inviting. I went down to Bill's house on a Sunday morning. The two of us sat on the front porch looking out at the beautiful day, each of us suffering from a bad case of cabin fever.

"By God," Bill said suddenly, "Kenny, let's you and I take a couple of pistols, load up old King, go across the river, and get Johnny and go for a ride. How about it?"

I was already halfway out the door. I shouted, "I'll go get old King!"

King was half German shepherd and half black Lab, weighing in at maybe 110 pounds of solid muscle. Around the back of the house, King was jumping up and down, making his chain sing like a fiddle string. His eyes were beginning to fail, but he was still a tremendous specimen of a dog. I untied him. He bounded around the yard, then up to the old Packard, where Bill waited with the back door open. King lunged into the back seat.

Bill grinned. "All set, son?"

"You bet," I answered, and we were off.

We stopped in Winona at the Sommers' family home. By now, Grandma Sommers had been dead a couple of years and Johnny lived there alone.

"Brother Bill, Kenny, come on in," Johnny greeted us at the door. "I see you've got old King in the car. What's up? Gonna take a hike?"

"Yeah, it's too nice to sit in the house today," Bill answered. "Thought we'd go down in Hidden Valley, see how the Sandstone Hole and the rest of it looks this year."

Sandstone Hole? Where have I heard that before? My mind raced back. *Yes! Yes! That's where Johnny caught those trout!*

We loaded up, Bill and Johnny in the front, me and King in the back. The ride to Hidden Valley took perhaps half an hour but seemed like an eternity. Finally, we were there. We parked in a little grassy opening alongside an old gravel road. After putting on our rubber boots, we found some walking sticks and began our springtime odyssey.

A dry wash full of rocks ran under an old, twisted iron bridge. We crossed the bridge, then followed a foot trail downstream along the crick bed. The wooded hills on each side seemed to crowd the wash into a zigzag pattern. Our pace was slow and easy. The early spring air smelled like sweet, heady perfume.

The wash ran alongside a small, rock-faced cliff. Here, Bill and Johnny set up a couple chunks of driftwood, then tried their hand at hitting them with their pistols, while I sat to the rear on a sandstone rock. As the shots rang out, old King's ears perked up. I held on to his collar to quiet him as he recalled days spent hunting in the duck marshes, when gunshots meant work.

Once again, we took up our walking sticks and headed down the valley. The valley floor here was about two hundred yards across, with hills on either side. At the base of the north hillside, a trickle of water appeared. Within the next five hundred yards, a profusion of springs flowed, crystal clear, bubbling and gurgling along the valley floor. Watercress grew in the springs like I had never seen it grow before. Great green water gardens lined the path of the sparkling spring waters. Everywhere was rock and gravel interspersed with small grassy meadows filled with wild violets. Huge basswood trees shaded the valley floor like a great awning.

We sat down on a big log. King cast to and fro, smelling and peeing at will. Johnny and Bill explained how this was the head end and fall spawning ground for all the valley's trout. We had walked at least a mile from the car. No wonder this crick was hard to find.

We sat, talking and laughing, sometimes all of us still as we listened to the spring birds sing their songs of joy. A red-tailed hawk glided above the hills, turning one way and then another, like a kite on gentle breezes. We shared some sandwiches with King, then knelt and drank heartily from the springs. The water was sweet and pure.

"We'd better get going," Johnny murmured. He stood and stretched his back. "We've got a long way to go."

The trail crossed the crick, then a stretch of woods, then back across the crick. We traveled in a fairly straight line, while the crick wound back and forth from one hill to another, as if the hills were a magnet drawing the water first to one hill, then to the other. The sandstone cliff rose thirty feet above the crick, then sloped away and up the bluff.

We reached a pool that stretched lazily downstream for forty feet with little current. Johnny told me to go downstream, below the pool, cross the crick, then work my way slowly upstream until I could sit on a flat sandstone ledge hanging over the pool.

I reached the ledge and sat down. From the ledge upstream, perhaps thirty feet, several half-submerged sandstone boulders created a heavy riffle. The water depth varied from about three feet at the head to around five feet below the ledge, then flattened out to a couple feet toward the bottom end.

Sitting there quietly, I saw trout moving in the clear water. Their bright colors startled me, yet at times blended in with the gravel and rock bottom. As I was about to leave, I noticed a large, squarish tail protruding from under the sandstone ledge.

Johnny called out, "Any good ones in there?"

"Looks like there's one for sure."

"There usually is." Johnny and Bill chuckled.

Downstream from the Sandstone Hole, the woods thickened. Several larger springs fed the crick. This stretch was composed of riffle–log–hole, riffle–log–hole for a half mile or more. The ancient trees had fallen this way and that, creating dark, cool pools with plenty of feed and cover. We saw few trout. Most, I imagined, were hiding under the logs. I ached to drift a line under the shadows. The soil in the Big Woods was rich, dark, and moist. We found several patches of skunk cabbage. I pinched off a leaf and inhaled the pungent odor of plant and soil.

A barbed-wire fence separated the wild part of the valley from the tame part. Downstream from the fence was a cow pasture.

Farther downstream, the valley floor widened considerably. Here, the crick banks were higher, the crick, wider and shallower. Strangely enough, the crick bottom was still solid gravel. Half a mile downstream from the fence, a long, sweeping bend in the stream arched the water toward the eastern hillside. Here, we found part of an old stone building foundation and the remnants of a grinding wheel.

We sat down to rest in the afternoon sun, and Johnny and Bill filled me in on the history of the Old Mill. Many years ago, settlers built a water-powered mill here to grind their grain and corn into flour and cattle feed. A rough-hewn road ran down the steep bluffs to the mill. The farms were located on the bluff tops because the valley floor was too narrow and rocky to cultivate. When the farmers drove their horse-drawn wagons down to the mill to grind feed, they most likely filled their water barrels as well. Then, one spring day in the early 1900s, a great flood rushed down the valley, causing the stream to change its course. The farmers had no choice but to build another mill on the opposite side of the valley.

We looked across the valley and saw part of another foundation. Bill said a couple of grinding wheels were lying there, too.

The sun felt good as we sat by the mill ruins. My eyes grew heavy as I listened to the rushing water. My mind filled with visions of men wearing straw hats and bib overalls, perched on wagon seats and driving teams of horses down the bluff road. In the wagon was cob corn, sacks of grain, and several wooden water barrels jostling about. A couple of dogs loped behind the wagon. The horses' leather harnesses creaked, and the wooden wheels squeaked and clunked over the rocky road. Now and then, the man talked to his horses: "Easy now, Queenie. Hup there, Belle."

The bark of a dog, far atop the hills, woke me from my dream.

"Let's go down to the Willow Tree Hole," Johnny said.

Another ten-minute walk and we were there. Along one side of the hole ran a steep, eroded bank about five feet high. On the other side, the bank gradually merged with the water. We approached from the gentle side. A fast riffle fed in upstream. The hole was deep and bluish black. From the center, where it was deepest, emerged a huge root, willow branches splayed out to all sides. We sat at the edge of the water, watching a few small trout rise for flies in the shallows.

Suddenly, old King plunged headlong into the pool, water spraying in all directions. He swam around the hole, then climbed out and shook off, giving us a shower.

"Well," Bill said, "I guess that's the end of the trout-watching in the Willow Tree Hole." We all laughed.

A cow path led from the pool down through the pasture. In the distance, a grove of trees stood on the valley floor. The crick meandered between the trees. A small herd of cows grazed contentedly in the grove. Bill decided we'd better turn back before King got mixed up with the cows. Reluctantly, we headed back upstream, stopping now and again to gaze into the crystal water or to look at wildflowers.

About halfway through the Big Woods, we crossed the widest and steepest spring that fed into the main crick. We followed the spring fifty yards to where it bubbled out of the ground. A thick carpet of moss covered the rocks and ground. The moss was cool to the touch. Marsh marigolds and watercress grew in huge patches. My God! What a beautiful place.

Johnny produced two plastic bread bags from his hind pocket, took out his jackknife, and began cutting watercress. Bill and I joined him. In no time, the bags were full of cool, dark green watercress.

As we neared the car, the robins heralded the coming twilight. I turned and looked back at the valley. What I had heard, smelled, and seen during this beautiful day was stamped in my memory. Thus began a lifelong affair with Hidden Valley.

On the way home, King lay with his head on my lap, dreaming of stumps, water, and cow trails. I thought long and hard, *Should I or shouldn't I?*

Finally, I blurted out, "You think it'd be possible I could go trout fishing with you guys this year?"

Bill and Johnny looked at each other. The silence was deafening. At last, Johnny said, "I don't see why not."

I could have sprung through the car roof, but I held myself in check.

The next day, I bought my first Minnesota nonresident fishing license. A seemingly endless week followed. At last, Sunday morning arrived.

Johnny and I left the car by the iron bridge early in the day. Rubber boots, fly rods, worm boxes, bottles of hooks and sinkers, stringers, and sandwiches were all the gear we carried. I began fishing at the Sandstone Hole. I tossed my worm-baited hook into the pool below the ledge. I just knew in no time I'd have my limit of ten trout dangling from my stringer. After all, wasn't this crick teeming with trout?

Five minutes later, no bites. I pulled my line up and moved farther out on the ledge, throwing my bait farther downstream. In the deep, clear water at my feet, trout zipped back and forth, some diving for cover right under the ledge.

This time I waited maybe ten minutes. No bites. The line lay quiet, as if there wasn't a trout within five miles.

Oh well, I thought, *I'll just move down into the Big Woods where all those shady, dark log holes are. Surely I'll get some there.* I pulled in my line.

I figured Johnny, who had gone downstream ahead of me, would be a ways into the woods by now. But when I came to the first good hole, there sat Johnny, almost completely hidden in the shade behind the upturned roots of a fallen tree. His pole lay a short distance away, line sagging under the tree in the pool.

"Doing any good?" I asked.

"Got two so far," he answered.

I walked by, continuing down the crick to the next pool.

I drifted my bait under a log. Bang! My line straightened out. I reared back on the pole, felt the weight of a fish for a second, then slack. I baited up again, drifted my bait under the log a half-dozen times with no results, then moved on.

During the next several hours, I worked my way out of the Big Woods, into the pasture, past the mill ruins, and all the way down to the Willow Tree Hole. It was a nightmare. Either I didn't get any bites or I missed the ones I got. Finally, at the Willow Tree Hole, I landed a small trout. I held him tightly and put him on the stringer carefully, as if he were the first trout I had ever caught.

I thought of Johnny. Where in the hell was he? I hadn't

seen him since the morning. Maybe something had happened to him.

I started upstream at a brisk walk. I found him halfway through the Big Woods, sitting against a big basswood tree in a grassy clearing, pole at his feet in the grass, line lying quietly in the dark pool.

"How'd you do?" he asked.

I held the little trout out of sight. "Oh, I got one. How about you?"

"They're down there on the stringer." He pointed to a shallow, rocky riffle.

I went down to the riffle, took a good-sized rock off the end of the stringer, and pulled it up. Seven sleek, dark-backed trout flopped and splashed in the shallows! A couple were in the sixteen-inch class. My heart sank.

"Bring 'em along up here," Johnny called, as he wound up his line. "I guess we've got enough for today, huh?"

"I don't know about you," I answered, "but I sure as heck have had enough for today." I wound the stringer around my hand and started up the bank.

Johnny chuckled while he took his pole apart and fastened the two ends tight with rubber bands. "Some days are that way. Let's go up to the big spring to clean 'em." He led the way up the foot trail, me tagging along behind like a kid.

Damned if I don't have to carry his trout for him, on top of it all.

Upon reaching the source of the big spring, we knelt at the edge and cleaned the trout. We put the innards high on the bank so the critters could find an easy meal, scratched the blood lines from the backbones with our thumbnails, washed them carefully, then placed the trout back on the stringer and laid them in the bubbling current to cool. My little eight-incher lay on the same stringer with Johnny's beautiful catch.

With the trout undulating in the swift wash of the spring, Johnny and I settled back among the marsh marigolds, the watercress, and the soft moss.

Johnny slid his cap from his forehead. "Seems like you covered quite a bit of crick today, Kenny. Might wanna slow down a little next time. Sometimes in these clear-water cricks you've got to sneak up to the hole, ease the bait into the water, and wait 'em out, you know."

"Yah, I guess I didn't think that far today."

He smiled. "Any day spent out here is a good day, no matter if you catch trout or not."

We lay back in the afternoon sun. Johnny muttered, "Just listen to that water gurgle, the whisper of the breeze, and those birds singing. Ain't that purdy? It just don't get any better than this."

I looked down at my boots. I was suddenly ashamed. It was the first time all day I had truly heard those things. I had been so intent on catching trout, I'd missed the best part of the day.

* * *

From that day on, I spent as much time as I could with Johnny on the clear-water cricks of southeastern Minnesota.

When I wasn't fishing, I was dreaming about fishing. More was learned from watching and listening to Johnny, and studying the cricks and the trout in them, than I could have dreamed of learning elsewhere. Johnny never preached a lesson; he suggested it. The same was true of the streams and the trout. The lesson was there to be learned; I just had to watch and listen to find it.

Summer turned to fall, and with fall came the end of trout season and a sense of regret. Every year in late winter, a feeling of unrest came over me. By spring, I was chomping at the bit, eager to begin another season on the cricks, seeking the wary trout. Increasingly, I not only sought the trout but the companionship of my fishing partner, Johnny. Largely through him, the subtle joys of looking at plants, trees, and critters opened to me. I better appreciated the sounds of the water, the birds, and the wind. The smells of the earth after a fresh rain, blooming plants in midsummer, and the hint of fall in the air in late August took on new meaning.

Over the years, we branched out to new cricks, new states, and even some new fishing partners. "When you fish trout with someone," Johnny always said, "you take a pretty good measure of their character."

A case in point was the time Johnny, Bill, and I joined their uncles, the Bitzan brothers, for an opening-day trip to the Whitewater Valley. We decided to fish the south branch of the Whitewater River. Our destination was the biggest pool in the south branch, a place called the Priest Cottage Hole.

To reach the hole, we drove Curly Bitzan's Nash Rambler through a long, tree-studded pasture. The pasture "road" in spring gave new meaning to terms like "pothole," "chuckhole," and "sinkhole." After getting out of the car a dozen times to push, shove, and grunt, we finally arrived at the end of the road, some fifty yards from the Priest Cottage Hole. Someone mentioned to Curly that his Rambler wasn't even very dirty.

Curly snapped back, "Hell, it can't be dirty. We carried the damn thing in here!"

We all roared good-naturedly, including Curly.

Rocks were rolled into circles; fires started; frying pans, bread, bacon, and eggs were brought out; and soon the mud was forgotten. More fishermen were making their way to the Priest Cottage Hole. We heard the grinding gears, slamming doors, and swearing along the pasture road.

Ben Bitzan sat on a stump, a cup of coffee in his hand. "Guess we'd better stake out a piece of water pretty soon," he said.

Johnny, Bob Bitzan, and Del Bitzan crossed the stream below the Priest Cottage Hole, then spread along the bank where the big riffle emptied into the huge, dark hole. Bill, Curly, and I took up positions just above the big tree, where the water was quiet and slow.

People were arriving en masse now. Organized confusion ruled the day. Dogs barked and fought. Kids screamed and hollered, occasionally taking time out to throw a rock in the crick. Cars and jeeps tried to ford the stream below the hole, heading upstream to places like Blue Lake or Box Car Rock. About one in three got stuck at the crossing. A few of us would go down to push them out and wish them luck fishing. Above the noise, a woman's shrill voice screeched, "Damn it, Herman, you just slammed my rod in the trunk!" Along the steep banks of the Priest Cottage Hole, people jostled for a spot to stand and minnow buckets tipped over, sending their contents skittering into the water.

Curly stepped to the top of a boulder, wide-brimmed hat on his head and wire-rimmed glasses perched on the end of his nose. He held his big pocket watch in one hand and a fourteen-foot telescopic bait rod in the other. Suddenly, the pool became quiet. All eyes and ears tuned to Curly. According to a long-standing tradition, it was Curly's duty to announce the opening of trout season.

Curly raised his hand in the air. "It's ten a.m.," he shouted, "and the trout season has now begun!"

At least forty lines hit the water. Within moments, the first fat trout of the year was landed and then clenched in the hands of a youngster directly across from me.

So went the rest of the morning, everybody catching a trout or two, eating lunch, and probably taking as much enjoyment from people-watching as from trout-catching.

Ben, having seen more than sixty opening days come and go, summed it up best on the way home: "Opening day is when everybody gets the kinks out of their lines, their legs, and their minds, even though it's something akin to a three-ringed circus. In another month, the weeds and the bugs will be out in full force, then us 'real' trout fishermen will have the cricks pretty much to ourselves, but actually every person who goes fishing on opening day is a 'real' trout fisherman in their own way."

We nodded sleepily as the Rambler rumbled and bounced along the dirt roads leading out of the Whitewater Valley, knowing that if we felt like it, tomorrow we were free to pursue that most precious of all fish: trout. That was the real significance of opening day.

Even though Johnny and I spent countless enjoyable days fishing other streams with other fishing partners, we always returned to Hidden Valley when we wanted quiet and tranquility. We recharged our batteries there, striking out on our own for a day of solitude, then meeting at the Willow Tree Hole an hour or two before dark. From there, we'd amble past the Old Mill, into the Big Woods, and stop by the big spring to clean our catch and compare notes on the day. Rarely did we meet another fisherman. On the occasions I did come across another angler, I stayed out of his way, knowing that whoever came to this lonely valley sought more than just trout.

As the years passed by, Johnny and I made fewer trips to our special crick. His hair was now silver. Once a man who could walk with the best of them, Johnny now walked slower and stopped oftener.

One time when we were cleaning trout in that beautiful spot at the head of the big spring, Johnny said, "You know, Kenny, I love this place. The water is sweet, and it seems like it will run forever. I wonder if the same water ever comes back here again?"

"I reckon it will," I answered, "but who knows when?"

That was Johnny's last trip to the valley.

We fished together a few more times on easy-to-reach cricks. But arthritis had crippled Johnny's fingers and the spark was leaving his eyes. I guess I knew what was coming but I chose to ignore it.

It was a cold, windy February day when my wife came home from work and put her arm around my shoulder. "Uncle Johnny died last night," she said. "Dad found him sitting in his chair. I guess he just went to sleep and never woke."

That spring and every one since, I've made a pilgrimage to our beloved valley. Sometimes I take a pole; sometimes I don't. Always I follow the crick downstream, marveling at the wildflowers, listening to the birds, stopping often to look and listen and feel the springtime delights.

Yup, the old skunk cabbage patch is still here, by golly, I think, as I snip off a piece and put it to my nose, almost tasting the tangy odor.

On the ledge overlooking the Sandstone Hole, I sit in the sunlight and gaze into the clear water, looking but not really seeing, remembering the time I took that twenty-incher from under the ledge after a heavy rain. How proud I was that evening when I held it up for Johnny to see.

Now I'm in the Big Woods, sitting in the shade of the old basswoods. How they whisper in the breeze! The water in the log pool is dark and foreboding. A fine scum rests against the upstream edge of the logs. How long have they lain in their watery grave? Two red-tailed hawks soar on silent wings; around and around they go. Are they related to the hawk we watched on my first trip here more than forty years ago? I'd like to think so. A splash in the scum breaks the spell. I look down to see ripples where a trout took a fly.

On to the pasture and the Old Mill foundation. I sit on a rock fallen from the foundation, looking across the green, pastured valley to the other mill site, wondering if the crick will ever shift again. I suppose it will; all things change with time. To my left, a bull snake is stretched out on a corner stone, enjoying the afternoon sun. My eyes meet his unblinking stare. How lucky he is, content with his life of eating, resting, and sunning. My thoughts turn to the folks who relied on this mill. Harder times but simpler and maybe happier, too. I wondered what they would say if they could see the world now.

One more stop: the Willow Tree Hole. Yes, it's the same, maybe a little shallower, but the great willow still lies in the

center as if anchoring the pool in place. Some trout rise for flies at the head of the hole. I turn upstream for the long walk back.

On the way back to the car, I stop often to rest. My left leg pains me. God, I used to walk that whole stretch with no more than one stop! I look down at my hands; the knuckles are swollen. I rub the backs of my hands along the sides of my legs, then continue with my journey. Near the car, I stop below the iron bridge and look down the valley. A meadow lark sings, then a robin. I turn reluctantly for the car.

Another summer is beginning in the valley. Another trip to Hidden Valley is over. I sit in the car, staring at the bridge.

I know that one of these springs I'll take this same walk. I'll visit all the familiar places. It will be twilight when I reach the Willow Tree Hole. There, sitting on the gentle, grassy bank, pole lying beside him, will be a familiar form, gray hair sticking out from under his cap, khaki pants and shirt sweaty and grass-stained. I'll go over to him. "Any luck?" I'll ask. "Oh, got a few," he'll chuckle. I'll reach down, pulling up the stringer and wrapping it around my hand. "Mmm, a couple of dandies." "They're all dandies out of this crick," he'll say. We'll walk upstream side by side, past the Old Mill, into the Big Woods, and to the head of the big spring. There, among the marsh marigolds and watercress, we'll clean the trout. We'll sit back on the cool moss, listening to the killdeer and the whippoorwill. In the gathering darkness, we'll sit together by the spring that runs forever.

THOSE LAZY, HAZY, CRAZY DAYS OF SUMMER

It was a hot, humid August afternoon when I sat in an old chair under one of the huge, twisted soft maple trees in my yard. A morning dove cooed its lonesome song from a branch. Now and then, a car or motorcycle roared past on the street. From the river came the whine of outboard motors. From several directions, dogs barked—now one, then the other, seemingly taking turns. I became increasingly aware of an unbelievable number of lawn mowers droning on and on and on. It seemed as though a hundred children screamed and chattered incessantly, like a great clan of monkeys. Just to give this audible assault some diversity, every so often a plane would fly over; some of the small ones circled over the river as if their controls were stuck.

To keep from going mad, I turned on the radio, foolishly figuring some good music might help. Before I heard a song, I listened to several commercials. One told me how to shrink hemorrhoids; another extolled the virtues of Fruit of the Loom underwear. I guess the two do go hand in hand, or would one say cheek to cheek? No matter, because soon a couple of boom boxes blared and bellowed their ghastly chant from the park. It was then that I summoned what little presence of mind I had left.

I found my way to my battered car, crawled feebly behind the wheel, took a big three-fingered dip of snuff, and started down the road. The four-mile drive to the swamp was a blur of assorted signposts, houses, kids on bicycles, and cars.

I must have made all the turns by instinct, because soon I was stopped in front of my old shack on the banks of Big Lake. As a rule, I use a canoe to travel the swamp, but not this time. No, I plunged headlong into the mud and water, making an entry that would have made any good Labrador retriever proud. I bulldozed through the cattail patches, half swimming, half walking, sometimes crawling. How long I wallowed in the marshes and swamps I do not know. The

Illustration by Bob Savannah, courtesy of the U.S. Fish and Wildlife Service

next thing I remember, I was laying facedown on a wooded island. When I stood up, a frog jumped out of my shirt pocket.

As I walked back to my car, an assortment of invertebrates crawled up and down my legs. I brushed them off as best I could. Now and then, I stopped to ponder the circumstances. The hum of mosquitoes and deer flies filled the air. It was the sweetest music I had ever heard. Several times, I encountered a water snake or a snapping turtle. How good it was to see my friends. A flock of ducks fed on the duckweed, gabbling back and forth among themselves. A blue heron gave his deep, raucous call as he took to the air. How soothing and natural the sounds of nature are compared to man's crazy inventions.

At last, I reached the shack. Upon looking in the mirror, I startled myself. I realize I'm no Robert Redford, but I struggled to recognize myself. Two inches of dried black mud plastered the top of my head, as though someone had administered a poultice. My face was streaked with mud, scratches, and bug bites. Some of the welts stood out half an inch. My clothes looked as if they had been marinated in axle grease. I looked at my feet and noticed one shoe was missing.

"Oh hell," I said, "I'll clean up when I get home." I took one last look at my beloved swamp, crawled into my car, and trundled down the road.

At home, I opened the fence gate and drove up by the little barn. I was limping down the driveway to close the gate when the neighbor lady and her young son, Jimmy, walked by on an evening stroll.

Jimmy immediately waved. "Hi, Kenny."

I returned the wave. "Hi, Jimmy, how ya doin'?"

"Oh, I caught three sunfish off the dock today," said Jimmy, and they were on their way.

I sat down in the old chair under the maple tree. As they continued down the road, I heard Jimmy say, "Ma, when I grow up, I wanna be just like Kenny Salwey."

"Jimmy," his mother replied, "you know Kenny Salwey's never amounted to a hill of beans. If it weren't for his poor wife working her fingers to the bone, and their friends and relatives helping them out, they probably would have starved to death a long time ago. It's downright disgraceful. Why, I don't think he's ever done a decent day's work, just hunting, fishing, trapping, and tromping around in that stinky old swamp."

"But dad says he'd like to live as free and easy as Kenny does."

"I just bet he would!" Jimmy's mom retorted. "He's got a lazy streak in him, too. Did you see how Kenny looked? My God, I don't think that man's taken a bath for two weeks. To top that off, the damn fool only had one shoe on."

"But Ma, Kenny knows all about walking sticks and sauntering through the woods and fishin' trout and digging roots and deer huntin' and—"

"Jimmy," his mom blurted out, "you're going to go to college and wear a suit and tie, and have a family and a nice house and amount to something. Now I don't want to hear another word about Kenny Salwey, you hear?"

From a distance, Jimmy whined, "But Ma. . . ."

The summer sun hung low over the wooded hills along the Mississippi. I pulled my old straw hat low over my eyes and dozed off. If you could have peered under the mud and the blood and the sweat on my face, you might have seen the corners of my mouth turn up, in the makings of a grin.

THE BULLFROG'S BALL

Some say it's Hell, but you never can tell
what the black swamps mean to you
'til you've stayed all night where there ain't no light
and the swamp's dark secrets come true.
Now the black swamps moan and sometimes they groan.
It's a strange concerto indeed.
But the bullfrog's song seems to drift along.
It's a tune we all sometimes need.

CHORUS
Papa did say you better mend your ways.
Quit dancin' at the Bullfrog's Ball.
When the bullfrog sings and other night things
begin to roam and give their call,
that's the time of night you wanna hold on tight
or you won't see morning at all.
Papa still does say better mend your ways.
Quit dancin' at the Bullfrog's Ball.

They set up a din, now the owls join in,
and the coyotes harmonize all.
On a black swamp night 'til first morning light,
we'll all dance at the Bullfrog's Ball.
But if we don't chance to get up and dance
to the tunes at the Bullfrog's Ball,
we'll lose something sweet and bound to repeat
mistakes that will cause us to fall.

REPEAT FIRST LINE AND THEN THE CHORUS

*Illustration by Charles Douglas, courtesy of the
Canadian Museum of Nature*

*Illustration by Bob Savannah, courtesy of
the U.S. Fish and Wildlife Service*

A Splash in the Night
A River Rat's Bear Tale

The waters of Solberg Lake were dark and angry. An ominous storm cloud cut by jagged lightning streaks boiled to the northeast of the lake. A distinct chill replaced the hot, humid air as the wind gathered strength from the approaching storm. Within minutes, roller waves crashed on the shore and the wind shrieked and howled through the tall pines and hemlocks ringing the lake. A deluge began. Sheet after sheet and wall after wall of water pounded the windblown landscape. Nature was showing its power.

I was mighty thankful to be sitting at a picnic table under the roof of a shelter. Even under that cover, I had to move to another table because of the rain blowing into the open-sided building. My thoughts were with the birds and critters. Where could they possibly find shelter from such an onslaught? And how about the folks camping in tents scattered throughout the nearby forest? Wow! I bet they were hanging onto their tent poles for dear life!

I had been invited to do a nature talk at Solberg County Park near Phillips, Wisconsin. My contact person was Butch Lobermeier, the Price County land conservation chief. I was waiting for him when the late July storm struck.

It was still blowing and raining hard when he arrived. Butch introduced me to his wife, Mary, and we talked a bit about the storm. They asked if I wanted to camp overnight in the park. I allowed as how I wasn't too fond of neighbors when I camped. I said I'd rather go to some dead-end trail in the woods for the night. They offered me their spare bedroom, but I declined, confessing that this old river rat was too shy and self-conscious to spend the night in the home of someone I'd just met. No, I'd go out in the woods, put down an old Army poncho, crawl into my bedroll, and sleep peaceably to be sure.

Mary gave Butch a wondering sideways glance and shook her head, then the three of us went about setting up tables and chairs for my talk.

Given the weather—it was still blowing and raining at a good clip—I thought a good-sized group assembled for my talk. I had a wonderful visit with those folks. We exchanged many stories and palavered for some time after my talk was over. By now, the rain had ended, but the wind still blew.

Butch and Mary helped me load my gear into my truck. I was to follow them to my "designated campsite." After several miles of blacktopped county roads, we turned onto a two-wheel-track dirt road that led into the dark forest. During the next mile of travel, several blown-down trees lay in the road; we squeezed past by the skin of our teeth. The road was littered with water puddles and branches the whole way. At last, we stopped in a clearing at the trail's end.

At the clearing, the three of us formed a semicircle in front of the trucks. Butch explained that this area was some sort of river flowage. An earthen dike ran alongside what looked like a long, narrow lake.

"That there is some high ground," Butch said, shining his flashlight on the dike. "Should be a good place for you to sleep, don't you think?"

I agreed wholeheartedly and said I figured I'd sleep there just fine.

As the aftermath storm winds blew through her hair, Mary looked incredulously at me, then at Butch. "I can't believe we're doing this," she said. The look on her face indicated that she felt she was the only one of us with both oars in the water.

"Aw, heck, you'll be okay, won't you, Kenny?" said Butch as he slapped me on the back.

Once again, I agreed 100 percent.

Mary must have figured this was some sort of a man thing and gave up her protest. The three of us shook hands. Butch and Mary started their truck, and their taillights disappeared down that dark, lonesome trail.

I busied myself in the back of my truck. Soon I had my duffel bag, water bottle, and flashlight in hand. It was as dark as the inside of a roadside culvert as I made my way through the tall, wet grass toward the high ground on the dike. At least there won't be any water puddles up there, I mused.

On top of the dike, I stomped down an eight-foot-square place in the grass on a fairly level spot. I held the flashlight in my mouth and dug around in the duffel bag for my Army poncho. I spread the poncho on the ground. Next, I put down my sheepskin sleeping pad, then my sleeping bag. I was all set. It had been a long day. There wouldn't be any insomnia tonight. I crawled into my sleeping bag, put my arms under my head, and lay there. The wind had quit. It was dead quiet.

One minute, I was counting sheep jumping over the fence; the next minute, I was awakened by a sound. I listened closely. Far off down the flowage, a barred owl sang its eerie song. That wasn't it. I listened some more. A splash. Might be a fish. Another splash, then another. Something was walking along the water's edge not more than twenty feet below me. I reckoned it was a raccoon. I fumbled for my flashlight and brought it to bear on the source of the splashing. There, standing in the shallow water not more than a half-dozen good jumps of a squirrel from me, was a bear.

I had brought the light to bear all right, and this was the biggest, blackest, fattest bear I had ever seen in my life! Granted, where I came from, a couple hundred miles southwest along the banks of the Mississippi River, there ain't a whole lot of bears. But there are some, and I had crossed paths with a couple over the years. Either the ones I'd seen before were small or maybe they just weren't as "up close and personal." All I wanted was for me and the bear to part company right now! It dawned on me that it would be easier for my newly found friend to leave than it would be for me, seeing as how I was lying in a zipped-up sleeping bag surrounded by tall grass.

The bear looked directly into the flashlight beam, which meant it looked directly at me. I could have sworn those eyes glowed like two red-hot coals. I half-expected a vicious roar to come bellowing out of its throat. I say "its" 'cause I had no idea what this bear's gender was and I didn't want to find out. The bear didn't roar, but if it had, I would have found out how fast I could run in a zipped-up sleeping bag through tall wet grass in the dark while looking over my shoulder—not a pretty thought!

I stared at the bear; the bear stared at me. I turned off the light. Once again, it was pitch black. I was all ears, to say the least. After what seemed like an eternity, the bear slowly splashed along the shore, away from me and the truck. This was a good turn of events. I held my breath so I could follow the bear's progress.

When the splashes ended, I figured the bear was a long way off or had taken to land. In either case, it was now or never. I could stay where I was and hope the bear didn't return—which would probably make for a restless night's sleep. Probably? Let's face it: The thought of staying where I was never entered my mind.

In a flash, I was out of the sleeping bag. I crammed my poncho and sheepskin pad into the duffel bag. No careful folding going on here. No sirree, Bob. Time was of the essence. I was afraid of turning on the flashlight for fear it would draw the bear back. I couldn't see my hand in front of my face so it was all done by feel. It was a cramerama of magnificent proportions. I couldn't get all the sleeping bag stomped into the duffel bag so half of it dragged behind me through the tall wet grass. On the way to the truck, I stopped a time or two to listen. Surely I wouldn't run into another bear, would I?

Finally I had my hand on the handle of the truck's topper door, which was thankfully unlocked. I always have trouble unlocking that darn thing, and tonight I don't think my nerves could have stood it. In about three seconds, my stuff was in the truck and the door slammed. Surely I set some sort of gear-packing record.

I got into the truck, started the engine, and sat there shaking and shimmying and shivering and quivering.

In a few minutes, I said to myself, "For God's sake, man, get ahold of yourself." After a while, I began to see the humor of it all and actually chuckled a little to myself—very little, but some. I was a grizzled old veteran of countless nights spent alone as a subsistence hunter and trapper in the Whitman Swamp. I'm the Last River Rat. I began to shame myself. Here I was running and flopping around in the dark like a beheaded chicken on account of a little old bear. Well, maybe it was a big old bear that was so close I could hear it breathe, but nevertheless, I wasn't gonna get run out of my "designated campsite" 'cause of a little thing like that.

I shut the motor off, rolled the windows down a bit, kicked the seat back as far as it would go, and leaned back to rest my tangled nerves. The moon played hide and seek behind bulky, dark clouds. As the clouds came and went across the face of the moon, my eyes grew heavy. I drifted into a deep and restful sleep.

Some time later, a dream seemed to come over me. I felt the sensation of movement. A gentle rocking, an undulating feeling, up and down, back and forth, like being in a canoe on wavy waters. Slowly, my sleep-filled mind woke up. I sat up and peered, bleary-eyed, out the truck windows.

Out the truck windows! Jumpin' Jehoshaphat! I wasn't in any canoe and there wasn't any water. It was my truck moving up and down! What in tarnation! I switched on the headlights.

There, rubbing its rump on my front bumper was that same big, fat old bear. The bear rubbed a few more seconds, then walked away a few steps, turned and looked back over its shoulder as if to say, *There just ain't no peace anymore in the Big North Woods. I was out lookin' for groceries and got a big light shined into my eyes—almost fell over in the water. Then I found a wonderful rubbing post and durned if I didn't get two big lights shined on me. It's getting to where a bear can't even itch its butt in peace around here anymore.*

Clearly perturbed, the bear walked off, almost shaking its head from side to side. The bear and I had one thing in common: We were awful sick and tired of one another, at least for tonight.

They say that discretion is the better part of valor. To heck with valor; it was discretion time for me! The North Woods belonged to the bear. I headed south and there was no uncertainty about that.

I cranked up the old truck and headed out. Somewhere along that dirt road I could have sworn I saw a big, fat old bear standing on the shoulder. When I got there, it was only a blown-down branch full of leaves. Was I getting paranoid?

A ways down the highway, I stopped for gas. When I came out of the gas station, I thought there was a bear sitting on the hood of my truck. It turned out to be a stocky man wearing a black coat pumping gas on the far side of my truck. I had bear fever. It was time to get home and that's where I went, pronto!

Now I have had about every kind of outdoor adventure a subsistence river rat can encounter during forty-plus years of Mississippi River backwater travels. And I sure enough wasn't scared of the nighttime in the woods or of any of the critters that shared it with me. However, back at the end of that dead-end trail on a dark and windy night, a big black bear showed me who was boss in the deep North Woods. I now have a whole lot of respect and admiration for those beautiful, burly bruins.

And that's the way the river rat's bear tale went down.

The Redemption 'Coon

The skinny pup looked up at Mary Kay with a lonely stare as she drove by. He sat in the grader ditch alongside the back road, obviously dumped there by his former owner. It was more than my wife-to-be could stand. She backed up and parked near the pup. She talked to him for awhile, then lifted him out of the goldenrod and stinging nettle. She set him on the seat of her pickup truck and they drove off together. It was the beginning of a lifelong, inseparable relationship.

Mary Kay took the pup to her farm, fed him—he ate ravenously—and gave him a good drink of water. Then she loaded him back in the truck and set off for Buffalo City, Wisconsin. Four and a half hours later, she pulled up to my front gate.

I was skinning muskrats in the attic when my black Lab, Spider, began to bark. A car door slammed. Spider and I hurried down the steps to greet Mary Kay. She stood on the sidewalk, beaming, with the darndest-looking pup in her arms.

"Look what I found!" she exclaimed.

I looked but couldn't believe my eyes. Cowering in her arms was the most pitiful pup I had ever seen. To say he was thin would have been an understatement. His hide stretched drum-tight over his skeleton. His eyes brimmed with fear. His ears and feet and tail all looked five sizes too big for his body.

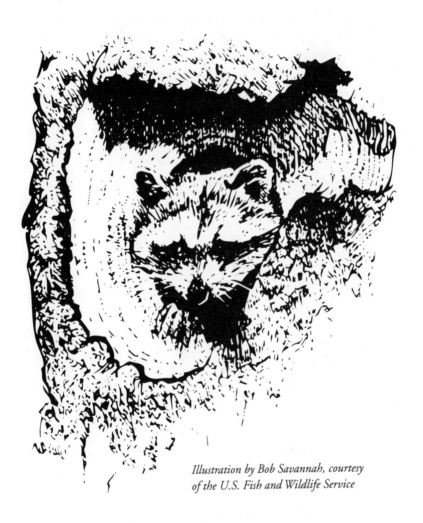

*Illustration by Bob Savannah, courtesy
of the U.S. Fish and Wildlife Service*

Mary Kay set him down on the sidewalk. He dashed away from me and crouched between her feet, shivering violently. She smiled. "The poor little guy needs a home. I just couldn't leave him out there to die. We can keep him, can't we?"

I took another look at the quivering brown ball and said the three words I would come to regret from time to time over the coming year: "Sure we can."

I had just broken a rule of thumb that had served me well over the past thirty-five years as a Mississippi River woodsman: one dog at a time!

Now we had two dogs in the car, two dogs on the trout stream, two dogs tagging along in the hills, two dogs in the house, and two dogs at the vet's, not to mention two dogs in the canoe. But I just couldn't say no to Mary Kay or to the pup—or to my own heart, for that matter. So began a year of high hills and deep, dark valleys. On the hilltops, we experienced much happiness. In the valleys, we found the kind of frustration that comes straight from the milltails of Hell itself!

Since we called our six-year-old Lab "Spider," Mary Kay decided to name the new pup Webster. We got to calling him Wee Willy Webster or Webby or Weber—all of which he generally ignored.

We tried to teach Webster to retrieve, using the time-honored methods of walking away as he brought the dummy back, putting a check cord on him, or letting him watch as

Spider retrieved the dummy. Each method brought little or no success.

At one point, Webster took a notion to stop riding in the car. Every time we went away, we would call to him, first pleading, then demanding. We even offered him doggy treats from the car door—no luck with that either. We finally resorted to manhandling him into the car.

A busy county road ran within a couple hundred yards of Mary Kay's farmyard, and we feared letting the dogs run loose when we were both gone from home. Tying them outside did not appeal to us, nor would it sit well with Spider and Webster, seeing as neither of them had ever been on a chain. Putting the dogs in the house would have been an okay option for Spider. However, we had visions of Webby "exploring" a hundred and fifty different things in the first hour we were gone, only to find the inside of the house looking as though a troop of wild monkeys had been there when we returned.

So we decided to build a foolproof pen for the dogs. After several days of sweeping and cleaning a calf pen in the old barn, we put down plenty of fresh straw, encircled it with chicken wire, and equipped it with a blanket, food, water, and rawhide bones. Now we had a good pen.

The next morning, we put the dogs in the pen. Mary Kay went to work; I went to run some errands in town. When we returned that evening, Webster was on the outside of the pen looking at Spider on the inside. He had chewed a hole right through the chicken wire! Over the next week, we added two more layers of chicken wire, another board on the bottom of the gate, and hay bales around the whole thing. That dog pen looked like a miniature Alcatraz. Every night, we found Webster on the outside looking in at Spider. He bounded over to us with whines and yelps—overjoyed that "Mom" and "Dad" were home. We abandoned the modified calf pen idea.

Next, we tried the corncrib. This wooden outbuilding had a crib measuring twenty-five feet long by eight feet wide, with three-inch spaces between the boards. Another three days of remodeling and we had a perfect, foolproof pen complete with doghouse, blankets, water, food, and rawhide bones, plus an assortment of squeaky toys. Mary Kay and I stood back to admire our handiwork.

That evening, after we arrived home from our daily jobs and errands, Webster was on the outside looking in at Spider! As far as we could tell, he had climbed onto his doghouse, then jumped up and scrambled over the six-foot door wedged in the far end of the crib. After fortifying that escape route, we found Webster, again, on the loose. This time, he had chewed a hole through the one-and-a-half-inch planks nailed to the sides of the crib! Wee Willy Webster was proving to be an escape artist to match the skills of Harry Houdini. The corncrib days were over and done with.

Webster grew up lean, lanky, and sinewy. He stood almost as tall as Spider but weighed only half as much. Grow he should have, seeing as how his diet consisted not only of dog food, but four or five pairs of Mary Kay's sneakers, one of my bait boxes, parts of two dustpans, the end of a broom handle, the ceiling of my "new" old car, six or seven dummies, a couple bites out of Mary Kay's hundred-dollar-plus Australian shearling boots, dozens of shirt buttons (we learned to put our dirty clothes in a closed clothes hamper), and, for dessert, the stuffing from one arm of a wingchair. To say Webster was a chewer was like saying J. Paul Getty had a little money!

When late October rolled around, Webster had been with us about a year and made good progress on all fronts. He now retrieved from both land and water with some degree of regularity. The breakthrough in Webster's retrieving skills came after a long patience-straining evening of throwing dummies in a field next to the barn. Webby would run out to the dummy, sniff it, and leave the retrieving to us. Mary Kay suggested we tie some feathers to the dummy. We went over to the nearby haymow to pick up some pigeon feathers. We tied them to a dummy and threw it just outside the door. Webby bounded to it, picked it up without hesitation, and brought it to our feet. He jumped up and down, begging us to throw it again. We did and Webby retrieved it. No plastic or canvas for Webby. He wanted to smell and taste the real McCoy.

After that, we put some thought—rather than all effort—into Webby's riding-in-the-car problems. Each time we got him into the car, we took him to a place that was fun for him. We went down the road a short distance to a neighbor's hayfield for an hour of chasing grasshoppers. Or over to a nearby pond for an evening of panfishing. Webby loved to play in the water with the fish on the stringer. Or out in the hills to a crick-side meadow for "frogging expeditions." Before long, "kennel up" was all we needed to say and he hopped into the truck with delight. We even had to be careful about opening the car door in the yard. Webby would jump in and refuse to come out.

Our troubles were over, at least on those two fronts. By the fall, Webster was steady to shot and loved to hunt gray squirrels in the woods surrounding Big Lake Shack. Mary Kay was a steady-handed, crackerjack shot with a .22. She and Webby made an awesome team. With Webster's speed, he could put a squirrel up a tree pronto. Then he would circle 'round the tree, looking into the branches, and bark excitedly. A sharp crack from Mary Kay's rifle brought the squirrel tumbling down to land on the ground with a *kaplop*. Webster was on it in a flash, growling as he mouthed it. Sometimes he brought the squirrel to Mary Kay. Sometimes he left it where he found it. Other times he brought his prize into the thickest tangle of brambles in the area, leaving the final retrieve to Mary Kay or—if Mary Kay was lucky enough to have her along—Spider. Always, Webster wore a grin on his dark brown face. The team brought many a fine squirrel dinner home that fall.

Webster not only progressed in the world of hunting but in the world of canoeing. As a matter of fact, he became quite the "canoe jockey." From the riverbank, he could leap six feet and land dead center behind the bow without so much as a jiggle of the canoe. Spider, sitting at her place of honor in the bow, would turn to me as if to say, *He ain't suppose to do that, is he, Dad?*

"It's okay, Spider," I'd murmur, "it's okay. Good boy, Webby, good boy." The first couple of times Webster performed that trick, I 'bout swallowed my snuff and my heart skipped a beat, but I came to realize that Webster had near-perfect balance and was as light as a feather on his feet.

Autumn turned to winter and we began trapping muskrats, beaver, and mink in the delta of Buffalo River country. One frosty, mid-December morning, Spider, Webster, and I drifted down the Buffalo River checking our trap line. Fresh snow had fallen overnight. Slush ice in the river made for tough paddling, so I beached the canoe and set out on foot across the ice-covered marsh. I pulled a sled to transport any animals we might catch. Our destination was a beaver colony a half-mile away. Not a cloud lingered in the azure sky. A south wind blew and the day promised to warm up by noon. The snow squeaked underfoot as if complaining about being disturbed. We seemed surrounded by a million sparkling jewels as the sun's rays touched each snowflake. Our breath looked like tiny puffs of smoke frozen in midair. Webster was his usual self, overdosed with energy, running circles around Spider, snow flying from his feet as he leaned into ever tighter turns—closer, ever closer to Spider until bingo, he grabbed her ear as he flew by.

Spider turned back to me. I patted her head and said a few comforting words. She always tolerated Webster's antics, like she had adopted him as her son or little brother. Who knows, but she's sure been long on patience.

In a channel leading from the beaver lodge to the river, I checked my first trap. I had set a body-gripping 330 Coni-bear there. The ice had frozen over the hole, so first thing, I chopped a small hole in the ice above the trap. I lowered the ice chisel down the hole until I felt fur. Next, I chopped out the trap stakes. Then I put on shoulder-length rubber trapping gloves and cleaned out the ice chunks from the hole.

Finally, I reached under the ice, took hold of the chain, and pulled the trap and beaver onto the ice. Wow! A black beaver and a mighty big one, too! I removed the trap and rolled the beaver in the snow to dry its drenched fur. Webster and Spider sniffed it out. They circled and barked at it a time or two. I sat down on an old beaver-cut stump to admire the animal's long, dark guard hairs glistening in the sun against the frosty white snow.

Land sakes alive but that's a beautiful critter, I thought. *Think I'll tan him and ask Mary Kay to hoop the pelt for a decorative wall hanging.*

The wind sang its song in the dry marsh grasses. A crow joined in a long way off. My thoughts turned to the Circle of Life and Death, how they are one and the same. They always entwine. One needs the other to keep the circle turning smoothly. Without death, there would be no new life.

But enough daydreaming! I returned to the hole and reset the trap. It took awhile. I had to hold it in the water to melt the ice off it. Then I lay down on my belly to set the trap on the channel bottom. I pushed the dead tree-limb stakes firmly in the mud to hold the trap solid. I added a few "guide stakes" to steer the beaver into the trap, and it was done.

The whole thing took probably ten minutes. After getting on my feet, I brushed the snow off myself and turned around. Webster stood next to the beaver with that hand-in-the-cookie-jar look, licking his lips. I walked over, or maybe ran—things were a little foggy right then—thinking, *He ain't chewed nothing much up lately, surely he wouldn't . . . he couldn't . . . he didn't. . . .* I looked down. He did! There in the middle of that beautiful big black beaver's back was a hole half the size of my hand.

I didn't know whether to laugh or cry. So I shouted: "Webster, you little diabolical chicken-lipped monster! Why did you chew a hole in this beaver? Come on over here! Come here, Webster!"

He did, and I pointed at the beaver. "No, no, no! Don't you ever do that again, you hear me? You little pot-lickin' varmint!"

Webster trotted off and sat down to watch my tantrum run its course from what he considered a safe distance. Spider stood looking back and forth from me to the beaver to Webster. *Boy, you sure did it this time, pal,* she seemed to be saying. *Dad's madder than a wet hen now!*

After further discourse as to the pros and cons concerning Webster's worth, I shrugged my shoulders and thought, *Aw, what's the use?*

I tied a rope around two of the beaver's feet, shouldered it, and carried the beaver back to the sled. It landed with a plop. We backtracked to the canoe as fast as we could go. Spider took the lead, and Webster brought up the rear a long way back. He had been mistreated by the former owner who dumped him in the country. He knew that human anger used to cause him pain. He never forgot that awful lesson.

Back at the canoe, we shared our lunch. I petted both dogs and we wrestled in the snow for a while. By then, all three of us were smiling and puffing happily. Forgiveness was given and received by each of us.

After lunch we canoed across the river, now ice-free, and traveled the open marsh to the north on foot. During the course of the afternoon, we caught about fifteen muskrats and one more beaver. This time, as I reset the trap, I watched Webby. Several times, he came within a nose-length of the beaver, sniffed it, and walked away.

"Good boy, Webby," I praised him. "That's the way, Webster."

Just before dusk, Webby barked a couple times. Then he growled and something growled back. I knew at once that Webster had found a 'coon.

He was out of my field of vision, so I crawled on top of a muskrat house. Again Webby barked and growled, and the 'coon told him in its own language to stay away. From my rooftop vantage, I saw them in the tall marsh grass along the Buffalo River, about seventy-five yards away. Between us lay a stretch of poor ice scattered with small, dark, open spots.

I began to pick my way over there as quickly as I could. Bad ice and failing light could go plumb to blazes. I knew just how tough an old swamp-wise boar 'coon could be around open water and a young dog. Webby getting a whuppin' was one thing. Webby drowning under the weight of a crafty old 'coon was another. If that 'coon had his way, he'd latch onto Webby's head and take him into the river for sure. Where the hell was Spider?

About halfway there, I heard her join the fracas and instantly felt better. Spider had "been there–done that." Man, was there ever a mêlée going on now. Barkin', growlin', snappin', snarlin', and squealin' all at the same time.

When I finally arrived, I had a hard time telling which one was the 'coon. Three balls of mud rolled in the tall grass at the river's edge. I finally sorted out who was who and got between them. A sharp wallop from my hunting axe to the 'coon's head ended it for good.

The three of us stood there for a couple minutes and breathed hard. Then I washed off Spider, Webster, and the 'coon in the river. I hung the 'coon on a tree branch, wrung out the water, and skinned it. It was a huge, gnarly, scarred-up old boar used to fighting for its life. All the while I was skinnin' the 'coon, Webster sat by my leg and growled. This was his first 'coon and he was proud of it. When the 'coon was skinned, we made our way back to the sled, packed up, and headed for home.

By the time we arrived home, the stars were twinkling and the moon was up. We were later than usual, and Mary Kay looked worried.

"What on earth happened to you guys?" she asked as her motley family trio trudged through the kitchen door, tired, wet, hungry, half-frozen, and muddy around the edges.

"It's a long story," I said. "I'll tell you about it over supper. Okay, honey?" Mary Kay nodded, and I went to change clothes and wash up.

After supper, Mary Kay and I joined the dogs in the living room. Webster lay curled on one end of the couch, Spider on the other. We sat between them in front of the fire. Mary Kay stroked Webster's head and murmured, "Webby, Webby, you're such a little rascal. I don't know what we're ever going to do with you!"

Webster just cocked one ear, nestled his head into the pillow, and sighed long and loud, as if to say, *What's the big deal? Stuff happens, Mom!*

We chuckled, shook our heads, and took each other's hand. Somehow, the fire seemed warmer and brighter, the smell of wood smoke and wet dogs more meaningful than ever before. Soon, our eyes grew heavy and, as I closed mine, I caught a glimpse of Webster looking up at me with one bright, piercing yellow eye. I knew in my heart that this vagabond's indomitable spirit would bring us many more memories, but none as vivid or meaningful as the day of the redemption 'coon.

Dusky and Red

The late autumn wind played a lonesome song among the naked treetops. Dead leaves whirled about the forest floor. Duck and goose talk filled the steel-gray sky as the wavering V's winged along the ancient pathways to the south. A flock of robins silently fed on the red fruit of a few scattered winterberry bushes. Soon, they would also take wing to their wintering grounds. I would miss my feathered friends. The river bottoms always seemed so quiet and uneventful without them.

I watched this scene from the west window of Big Lake Shack. Inside, a pot of wild-ginger and catnip tea steamed and bubbled atop the wood-burning stove. I left the window and poured myself a cup, then tossed a couple chunks of split oaks in the stove. On the bottom bunk, my dogs, Spider and Webster, snored rhythmically. Their chests rose and fell in peaceful slumber. No sense of loss there. No worries about the coming winter. No fears about tomorrow. Today was what counted, and today they had their bellies full, their bodies heated, a roof over their heads, and me close by. They needed nothing else.

That was simple living at its best. Why couldn't I be as content as they were? I knew I would carry on a "conversation" with them each day of the winter, but I still felt a void, a need for something more.

I returned to the window-framed forest, rested my elbows on the plank table, and sipped my tea. Outside, a

llustration by Charles Douglas, courtesy of the Canadian Museum of Nature

nuthatch busily examined the crevices in the bark of a great red oak standing near the fire circle. Above the first crotch in the tree, a red fox squirrel sat hunched against a thick limb, tail curled across its back for a windbreak, chewing on an acorn.

Aha, I thought, *I will have a winter guest after all.*

Out of the corner of my eye, I saw a black squirrel—black as coal, not another color on it—jumping from limb to limb. It had an acorn in its mouth. The black squirrel disappeared into a hollow in the tree.

The squirrels were a contrast in colors: red and black. These were the colors of the old-time woodsman. Red-and-black-checked wool clothes. Soft, silent, comfortable, fairly waterproof—exactly what was needed for survival in the woods. In fact, the very clothing I was wearing at the moment.

An idea formed in my mind. Why couldn't I feed the squirrels over the winter? Get to know them on a "personal" basis and have something else to visit during the longest and loneliest months of the year?

The next day, I headed east from Big Lake Shack to the farmstead of my old friend, Joe Greshik. Joe worked the farmland adjacent to the High Ground Woods. That year, he had planted corn a long stone's throw from my shack.

When I entered the farmyard, the door to the tractor shed stood open. The light inside was dim. Joe's voice boomed from the far corner:

"Kenneth, my friend, how's the world been treating you these days?"

"Fair to middling," I replied.

We shook hands and, after the fashion of river and hill-country folks, settled back to talk at some length about the year's crops, the river levels, whether or not any fish were biting, and what sort of wildlife we had seen lately. We sat on a couple straw bales, using the shed wall as a backrest. Taxes, politics, and other unimportant matters were not discussed.

"Joe," I finally said, "you've got a pretty fair stand of corn down along the swamp this year. Wonder if I might be able to pick a gunnysack or two full of it. Got a couple of real pretty squirrels living in that big red oak next to Big Lake Shack. Sure like to make friends with them if I could."

Joe looked down at his well-worn work shoes and shook his head. He turned to me with a smile. "Kenneth, every swamp critter and bird that loves to get its mouth around a kernel of corn has been working overtime in that field already. One more critter like you ain't gonna make a whole lot of difference. Go ahead, help yourself."

He slapped me on the back, and the deal was made.

I rambled back to the shack to ready my sacks. An hour or so later, Webby and Spider and I were in the cornfield. Joe wasn't kidding about the critters getting into the "grocery store." The first half-dozen rows all the way around the field looked as though they had been trampled by a young elephant with a case of wanderlust. Cornstalks lay across each other in every direction. It was a tangled mess and proved next to impossible to walk through.

While I picked as many full cobs as I could from that cornfield jungle, Webby and Spider ran in circles vacuuming the ground with their noses for the scent of the pilfering intruders who had created the great tangle. Now and again, one of the dogs would sort out the scent enough to send a squirrel or a rabbit scurrying for the nearby woods. None were caught, but that was okay. It was the chase that meant the most to Webby and Spider.

The setting sun found me with four large burlap bags full of dry, field-ripened cob corn. Enough for a winter's worth of squirrel feeding, I supposed, providing I could entice them to eat it. My plan was in my mind. Tomorrow it would be put into action. I could hardly wait.

The next day dawned crisp and clean. Jack Frost's night-time artistry covered the landscape. The breath of the River hung like a billowing white shroud above the Backwater Swamp.

I left the cozy warmth of Big Lake Shack with a corncob in one hand and a tin pail in the other. At the base of the red oak tree, I scanned the limbs for a sign of the squirrels. *Nope, not yet. They are probably sleeping late this frosty morning*, I thought. *That's what I oughta be doing myself.* I smiled at the thought of the squirrels curled inside the hollow tree, wrapped in their tails.

I tapped the corncob several times on the pail, shelled the kernels onto the ground at the base of the tree, and left it at that.

Inside the shack, I busied myself mending fishnet on the table next to the west window, where I could keep an eye on the corn and the doings of the squirrels. Every so often, I looked out to see a small pile of corn kernels, bright yellow against the fallen oak leaves. Maybe my plan wouldn't work.

Finally, I saw them. The fox squirrel led the way, coming headfirst down the trunk with the black squirrel close behind. They approached the corn cautiously. After close examination, they began to chew the centers out of each kernel and drop the "leftovers" on the ground.

The little devils would do that now, wouldn't they? At that rate, I'd be picking more corn in short order! Maybe when the snows came, their eating habits would become more conservative. Time would tell. For now, I was happy just to see them following the first part of my plan.

A routine developed. Each morning I would take the tin pail and a corncob to the red oak tree, where I would tap the cob on the pail—*tink tink tink*—then I'd shell the kernels onto the ground.

Back inside the shack, I would wait for the squirrels to come down and feed. My window-side eavesdropping didn't seen to bother them. In fact, after a week, I'd barely reach the window before they would scamper down to the corn.

Before long, I would tap the pail, shell the corn, and sit down on a stump chair not more than twenty feet away. The squirrels would come down and I could visit with them over their breakfast. With each passing day, the squirrels' trust in me increased. Exactly what I had hoped!

One evening, while I read by the flickering light of the kerosene lamp, what sounded like sleet began pelting the shack's tin roof. I poked my head out the door. Sure enough, there was hard water falling. Winter's first snow would come tonight.

Next morning, the woods were white. A half-foot of fluffy snow covered the ground. This would be a good time to try the next phase of my plan.

The last few days, the squirrels had been coming down the tree as soon as I tapped the can. It was like ringing a dinner bell. When they heard that sound—*tink tink tink*—they knew to come down for their free meal. Today, with the fresh snow and cold temperature, I figured the squirrels would be hungrier than usual. I knelt at the foot of the tree to clean away the snow, struck the tin can three times with the corncob, shelled some kernels into my outstretched hand, and waited.

In a moment, my little friends were on the ground beside me. They approached my hand with short, stiff-legged steps, noses twitching, eyes sparkling and blinking in the sunshine. The black squirrel was the first to pick a kernel from my hand. It sat on its haunches, held the kernel between its front paws, nibbled out the heart of the kernel, and dropped the "leftovers" back into my hand. The fox squirrel soon did the same. In a short while, they threw caution to the wind. Two small, cold, wet noses and two sets of long wispy whiskers were tickling my hand at the same time. I couldn't help but smile.

Over the next couple of weeks, I handfed them as often as I could, which turned out to be two or tree times on some days.

I also named them. The black squirrel became known as Dusky. The fox squirrel I called Red. Now each time they fed, I visited with them:

"Hi, Dusky, how you doing today?"

"Red, you look a little tired this morning."

"The sun was red when it rose. That will mean snow by tonight, my friends."

No doubt it was the corn that brought the squirrels down the tree to "listen" to me. But the corn brought them pleasure. To be sure, it was the visits that I was most interested in, so I guess you could say it was a win-win situation, like the lawyers tell it. It's been said that it's okay to speak to things that can't talk back to you, like dogs and trees and squirrels, as long as you don't answer yourself. However, at times, I did answer myself! But then I suppose that's about what you'd expect from a gnarly old river rat.

Dusky and Red, along with Webby and Spider, became my daily companions. The five of us made a happy little family.

Now and then, Webby would decide Dusky and Red were stepping on his turf. A quick rush on Webby's part would send the squirrels scampering up their den tree. They would scold Webby from a low-hanging branch, and Webby would return their insults by barking at them for a good long while.

One cold, snowy, mid-January day, while I was splitting wood near the edge of Big Lake, the scream of a red-tailed hawk pierced the air. The hawk dove into the upper branches of Dusky and Red's home tree. The hawk sat there for a moment, then flew away with empty talons. I breathed a sigh of relief.

That evening when I fed my little friends their supper, I shook my finger and told them not to sleep on the tree limbs during the day or Old Red-tail would have them for lunch. I also warned them to get to bed early. The night before, I had heard the hoot of a great horned owl. The owl would be looking for a midnight snack. It was the dead of winter and all wild things were fighting to survive. This was the natural way.

On the one hand, by giving Dusky and Red a steady reliable food source, I had made their lives a bit more secure and comfortable for the winter. On the other hand, by placing their trust in me, they were now more vulnerable to predator attacks from the air. Old Red-tail and Hooty the Owl both knew exactly which tree the squirrels lived in.

My fears for Dusky and Red's safety on the ground were not as great. Webby and Spider kept them on their toes in that regard. All I could do was keep my fingers crossed until springtime brought leafy cover to the den tree for my two friends.

At long last, the short days of winter gave way to the coming of spring in all its glory of promise. In mid-May, when the trees were lush with green leaves and the grasses grew tall and thick, some folks from Chicago came to the swamp. They wanted to photograph birds by canoe. I agreed to help.

We were eating lunch on a fallen log in the High Ground Woods when I mentioned my friends Dusky and Red. The birders were interested in getting some photos of me with the pair of squirrels. I said no problem, we'll do that this evening.

When evening came, the birders set up their cameras a short distance from the squirrels' den tree. I was confident the squirrels would behave as usual even though strangers were present. I fetched the tin pail and a corncob and sat by the base of the den tree. I tapped the cob on the pail—*tink tink tink*—and shelled some kernels into my hand.

In a jiffy, Red scrambled down the tree to eat. The birder's cameras clicked and whined but Red never batted an eye. It seemed strange that Dusky didn't come down. I told the folks we would try again in the morning. Dusky would surely be there then.

The next morning, we repeated the procedure with the same results. Red came for breakfast but no Dusky. Now I knew something was wrong.

Later that day, I went scouting for places to photograph birds along the shores of Big Lake. I was walking in knee-high marsh grasses when I came to a place where the grass was torn up and trampled down in a four-foot circle. A small, dark creature lay in a twisted position in the center of the circle. I stood in stunned silence, then dropped to my knees beside Dusky. I touched the small body. It was stone-cold dead. Fishing line was wrapped so tightly around the neck and chest that I had to cut it loose with my pocketknife. The other end of the line was caught fast to a tree limb hidden in the tall grass.

Anger flooded me. What thoughtless, disrespectful fool had thrown fishing line on the shore of Big Lake? After a moment, a hollow feeling made itself felt in the pit of my stomach. I knew who the fool was. Me.

Toward the tag end of summer, I had been coming to this spot to fish for bass. I recalled one hot, humid night when the bugs were making a pretty fair meal of me and my reel become a tangled ball of line. In frustration, I cut the line from the reel, dropped the line in the grass, and stomped away in disgust.

Now I asked myself over and over, *Why did I do such a thing?*

I picked up Dusky, and the dogs and I made our way back to Big Lake Shack. The fishing line was now stuffed in my pocket, where it should have been the night I cut it from the reel.

Behind the shack, Webby and Spider and I sat at the base of the squirrel den tree. I laid Dusky at the bottom of the tree. The dogs took turns smelling our little pal, then lay down to rest.

The evening shadows were growing long. In the woods, a robin told of approaching darkness. The ducks and geese gabbled in the rushes across Big Lake. From far away, an owl's call drifted on the breeze. There was so much life in the swamp this time of year. But all I could think of was death. I had killed Dusky in a slow and painful way. Tossing fishing line on a bank or throwing it over the side of a canoe was setting a trap not knowing what I would catch or when I would catch it. This action contradicted all the values I had learned from nature.

The backs of my weathered hands felt like sandpaper as I wiped the tears from my eyes.

I gained a sorrowful lesson that day. I will never forget what it cost me: the loss of a good friend.

Illustration by Charles Douglas, courtesy
of the Canadian Museum of Nature

A Fish Tale of a Fishtailin' Trout

My obsession with the monster trout began on an early spring day. It was mid-April and the south breezes blew warm. The snow had melted a week before. The first green sprigs of grass poked their lonely heads from the earth. The first robins of the year hopped about in search of the first worms. Oh Lordy, I had me a case of fishin' and spring fevers. Yes, and now it was time to catch the first firm, colorful trout of the year.

When I pulled into Dunk Davis's farmyard, an assortment of mixed-breed dogs charged the car, seemingly appearing from every nook and cranny. Some barked, some growled, and some wagged their tails. I opened the door and swung my feet to the ground. The dogs jostled for position to smell my boots; at least, I hoped they weren't fightin' to be the first one to taste my leg. Dunk opened the porch door and yelled a string of obscenities, and the dogs returned to their various positions about the yard. I walked up to the old farmhouse, shook hands with Dunk, and asked him how the winter had been.

"Christ, man, it was nothing but a nightmare!" he bellowed. "The weather was the direct opposite of Hell. Snow up to my butt. Lost three calves and half of my chickens! Most the winter we couldn't get out of the damn driveway either. How was your winter?"

"I was gonna say 'not too good,'" I answered, "but after I heard what you went through, I guess it wasn't all that bad."

Dunk laughed and took a three-fingered dip of snuff. "Wanna go troutin' down in my pasture?"

"Ya, I reckon I'd like to try it, if you don't mind." I took a good chew myself.

"You know the boy was down there late last fall, just before deer huntin'. He was a fixin' fence, see? Well, he come up on the high side of the old Cottonwood Hole, and by God, he claims he saw a brown trout as long as your arm and four times as big around." Dunk hesitated a moment to make sure I was listening. He needn't have worried—I could have heard a pin drop on a haystack five miles distant! He continued, "Now, I don't know whether he was a nippin' on the jug or what, but he claims it's the gospel truth, Kenny."

I was born and raised among the folks who live in the rugged hill country along the Mississippi River. These folks are as tough as the country they live in, so I, as a matter of course, took what old Dunk Davis had to say as the gospel truth.

Dunk and I looked at his cattle, discussed coon hounds to some length, and talked over the size of the turkey and deer populations. Finally, I left the farmyard to explore Dunk's cow pasture and the rocky, clear, spring-fed stream that wound through it for a mile.

"Name's Joey. She's had three litters of pups, twenty-seven pups in all, I guess, some good ones, too. She's thirteen years old in April. Been a huntin', trappin', fishin', and root diggin' with me every day! Best friend in the world."

Dunk pulled Joey's ear up. "See she's had her ear split once by a critter." He looked me square in the eye. "S'pose you're lookin' to go down in the cow pasture after that big fella in the Cottonwood Hole again, huh?"

My pulse quickened. "Reckon' I'd like to, Dunk, if you don't mind. Been after him about three years now. Ain't even had him on since that first time. Sure had some interesting times trying, though."

I launched into a story about a hot, humid night last August. "I'd been fishin' after dark when I heard the old trout slurp down a fly. I threw my crawdad toward him, but the line got hung up on a snag. I inched my way down the tree trunk, following my line with both hands. Next thing I knew, I slipped on some mossy bark. Would have done any logroller justice. Both my feet kept a churnin' but I kept going only one way and that was down. *Kersplash ka-plush*. I stood in water up to my neck, fish pole, line, branches, frogs, mosquitoes, and God knows what else all over me. My outburst of swearing must have been heard clear down to the end of the valley! After ten minutes of cuttin' line and breakin' branches, I drug the pole and my soaked hind end out on the stream bank. I sat there awhile, and darn it all if that trout didn't suck another fly down! I just shook my head, picked up what was left of my gear and my grace, and headed home."

The first trout of the year came flopping and splashing to the bank, fifty yards downstream from the Cottonwood Hole. I held it tightly in my hand, admiring the brilliant colors of the native brown. Then I slit the belly and cleaned the trout in the shallow riffles, throwing the innards high on the bank for a 'coon or mink to find on a night foray. I stowed my catch in a grain sack that I used as a fish bag.

Next, I eased up to the Cottonwood Hole. The sun shone at my back. I crouched down so my shadow wouldn't cross the water. I cast upstream maybe twenty feet. As the crawler drifted downstream toward the sunken cottonwood tree, I took up slack line. When the bait disappeared under the tree, a series of sharp raps tugged on the line. I gave the line some slack as the fish pulled the bait deeper under the sunken roots. I tightened the line. A heavy weight tugged back. I reared back on the fly rod as hard as I could.

All hell broke loose. The great trout bulldogged under the tree. The line hummed and whistled back and forth. My rod bent clear down to the water. The trout shot from his lair and broke water in an unbelievable spray of scum, water, and twigs. His mouth was agape, lower hook jaw twisting, red spots the size of dimes shining in the sun. I held a tight line and my breath. The crawler dangled from the corner of the fish's mouth—he was mouth-hooked, damn it all!

Again, the big fish broke the surface. This time, he stood straight up and fishtailed across the water, shakin' his head from side to side. The hook flew one way, the fish went the other, and my line went slack. My spirit did the same. My rear end found the edge of the bank and plunked down. With trembling hands, I cranked up the loose line. I examined the hook—nope, not straightened out, even got my crawler back. I chuckled at the irony.

The battle probably didn't take but a couple of minutes, but it seemed like half an hour. Everything had happened in slow motion. Three more ten- or twelve-inch trout found their way to my bag during the rest of the afternoon, but my heart wasn't in it. My mind kept going back to the Cottonwood Hole and the great fish that lurked in its murky depths.

Each year, as autumn wore into winter and winter turned to spring, that indelible picture of the great trout breaking the surface came to mind with more intensity until opening day found me in Dunk Davis's farmyard.

Dunk and I had what was almost a yearly ritual. We wouldn't see each other for maybe six or seven months, yet as soon as we shook hands, we took right off from there. We talked about everything from crops to politicians—politicians being one of our favorites.

"Hell, Kenny," Dunk said, "there ain't never been a politician yet who'd hold a candle to a good dog. A good dog is loyal, hard workin', and you always know about what to expect from him. Cain't say the same for them fellas now, kin ya?"

"You know what the trouble is?" I countered hate politicians. We just love dogs, that's all!"

We both laughed. I was itching to wet my lin I knew better than to insult Dunk by getting ar "business" of trout fishing before we'd finished visit. It was a hill country tradition not to be viol to settle myself down some.

Dunk shifted his tall, lean frame in the ricke swing. "How'd that white English hound turn ou I sold to your nephew Tim?" As he squinted in t sun, the crow's feet went clear back to his ears.

"Tim claims he's the fastest, toughest dog he e in his life."

Dunk grinned. "You know, some dirty bastar pup's mama right off the yard here last fall!" He "The buildings ain't much, but we got some thir There ain't a lock on nothing. Never was. We got geese, cows and calves, a few chickens, machine out. Nothing's missin'. Be damned if they woul man's dog, though! Lowdown, dirt-diggin' skunk that is." He spat vehemently.

"There ain't nothin' worse." I pointed to my sitting in the back seat of my battered car. "That hell on 'coons, too."

We ambled down to the car. Through the window, Dunk stroked the Lab's head.

"Female, huh? What's her name, Kenny?"

Dunk smiled and kicked my car tire. "Ya earned the right to try for 'im as long as ya wanna!"

Within twenty minutes, I had gathered my gear, donned my hip boots, rolled them down to the knee, and walked down the shady cattle lane to the high bank of the Cottonwood Hole. I stood quietly for a moment. A pair of killdeer bobbed and weaved along the edge of the sparkling spring. The water bubbled and gurgled down the center of the cow lane and emptied into the cottonwood deadfall.

I hooked a night crawler, as long as my hand and as big around as my little finger, once through the head on a number four hook. My cast sent it ten feet above the head of the hole, then it drifted downstream. The line went taut, disappearing beneath the two-inch coating of scum that floated against the deadfall. My heart skipped a beat. I knew what lay in the bluish black depths beneath the cottonwood. After the fish pulled the bait under the tree, I gave the line some slack. I laid the pole on the bank, making sure not to put the slightest hint of pressure on the line. Then I sat down and hummed the chorus of "Yankee Doodle Dandy" a half-dozen times. A little at a time, the slack line came to my quivering fingers. At last, the line was tight. I felt the weight of the fish.

"It's now or never," I murmured. I jerked the fly rod toward the sky.

The fish hugged the submerged tree. I felt him shake his head. He darted from the shade of the scum, swimming in a loose figure eight a couple of times, then surfaced. Again the old fish tried the same tactics that had won him his freedom the first time: He fishtailed across the water's surface, tiny silver beads of water spraying from his flanks.

This time the hook stayed put. I played him a short while longer, then he slid to the bank on his side. I picked up the beautiful twenty-six-inch male brown trout by the back of his head. The hook was out of sight in his gullet. My forefinger disgorged it. I cleaned him, then sat to admire him as he lay in the first fresh spring grass by the creek's edge. A drop of water traveled the length of his body, from head to tail, reminding me of a melting piece of ice on a hot summer's day.

I put the trout in my fish bag, crossed the creek, and stopped to gaze at the shallow waters in the tail end of the Cottonwood Hole. Guess I was giving thanks, after a fashion. To me, dreams and memories are the most precious creations of the human mind. My dream of catching the big trout had come true, and I still had the memories left.

I remembered the many days of pleasure the old trout had given me. I was drawn back to this valley, the lovely creek, its grand assortment of life. The anticipation of another chance at him. Sometimes the anticipation is sweeter than the reality. Many's the night I sat quietly alongside the Cottonwood Hole, sweating, swatting mosquitoes, and praying that tonight the monster trout would pick up my night crawler or chub tail, carry it under the tree, and swallow it. Day after day, year after year, I worked my bait downstream under the scum, then let it lie for long periods of time, only to go home without so much as a twitch of the line. But I'd go back the next night or the next week or the next year to try again.

I closed my eyes. The sights, sounds, and smells of the many spring and summer hours spent here came to mind: The frogs croaking and the crickets creaking. The killdeer at dusk, the whippoorwill after dark. Owls hooting back and forth from one hillside hunting-tree to another. Cows lowing as they grazed in the lush valley pastures. The far-off bark of the farm dogs guarding their homes. The scent of fresh-cut hay, catnip, basswood blossoms, and a hint of woodsmoke filling my nostrils. A haze of cool, moist air rising from the creek, sliding up, spilling over the banks, caressing my sweat-streaked face. How many times, while sitting by the Cottonwood Hole, had I seen raccoons foraging along the creek bank? A whitetail doe and her fawns eating along the edge of the hayfield? A V-shaped ripple in the still water of a muskrat or a mink making its way upstream? Ah yes, these things would all be here the next time I came, and someday another trout would grow big in the Cottonwood Hole.

A pair of wood ducks landed in the creek with a splash, ending my melancholy. I picked up my fly rod and made my way up to Dunk's farmyard, where I showed him my prize.

Over the next day or so, I showed my trophy trout to everybody I ever knew on this green earth—and quite a few folks I didn't know as well. I opened my ice-filled cooler so many times, I was afraid the hinges would fall off. I told and retold my fish tale of the fishtailin' trout.

Eventually I realized I had to do something more permanent with my fish. After kickin' around some ideas—ranging from mounting the fish to freezing it to taking some good color pictures to simply eatin' the thing—I opted for the eatin' side of things.

My brother-in-law Billy and I took up our fish spears and a flat-bottomed boat and went out in the springtime flooded river bottoms and got us some carp and buffalo fish to add to my catch. We cleaned and brined the whole mess in salt and brown sugar mixed with water in a Red Wing twenty-gallon crock. Right on the top, we placed my prized trout.

The next morning, we took the whole works to Grampa Dick Krause's farm, where we coaxed him into letting us use his hundred-year-old smokehouse. While Billy and I rinsed the fish and put them on the racks, Grampa Dick reminisced about how his dad had built the smokehouse out of home-sawed lumber. His eyes filled with pride as he allowed as how many a fine ham, side of bacon, and ring sausage had come out of that blackened old smokehouse.

We finished layin' the fish up, putting my big trout on the rack last. I couldn't resist telling Grampa Dick and Billy the story of my fishtailin' trout one more time. Billy and I heaped up plenty of good, green hickory wood, along with some apple limbs, under the racks and lit the fire. As we closed the door, I mentioned how good those fish would taste and we all heartily agreed, then we headed into the house for some of Grandma's cake and coffee.

Good conversation and eats make time slip away, and that it did until Billy walked past the kitchen window. He did a double-take and whirled around.

"The smokehouse is on fire!"

Did you ever see four people try to get through a narrow doorway at the same time? It ain't a pretty sight! Billy and I, being the youngest and strongest, won the squeeze-a-rama. We grabbed a garden hose—which we found out later wasn't turned on—and sprinted across the farmyard. Grampa Dick, being the oldest and undoubtedly the wisest, got tired of wrestling in the doorway, turned around, went to the telephone, and called the fire department.

After Billy and I spent a few moments running in place near the smokehouse, a siren sounded down the hill. The fire truck roared into the yard. A fireman jumped out, dragged a huge hose to the blazing smokehouse, and kicked the door in. Lookin' back, what happened next was akin to settin' off a dynamite charge inside that smokehouse: The fireman cut loose with all the water pressure they had in the tank.

Lumber, firewood, and fish flew everywhere, but mostly up. There were chunks and pieces, bits and tidbits. Some flew so high you could barely see 'em. Worst sight of all, though, was at the very top of that stream of water, standin' straight up and fishtailin' one last time, was that damned trout. If I didn't know better, I would swear that trout had a leering grin creasing his ugly hooked jaw.

The debris—at least most of it—settled back to the earth. A certain amount of its stayed atop Grampa Dick's tin barn roof. Billy and I cleaned up the best we could and left. The neighbors claimed they smelled burnt fish all summer as it melted off the barn roof.

In our Mississippi River hill country, news like that travels fast and it wasn't long before everybody and their uncle knew about Kenny, his fishtailin' trout, and the smokehouse debacle.

To this day, I'm asked questions like:

"Did you try to catch that trout on the way up or on the way down?"

"Have any blackened trout lately?"

"Would you wanna smoke me up a nice mess of fish? Hope you got your own smokehouse!"

I ask you, is it unreasonable for me to never, ever want to hear the words "fish tale" again?

Somethin' Fishy Goin' On

When we married, my darling man,
you said you'd always understand.
We'd have enough to eat and drink,
a house down on that easy street,
I think there's somethin' fishy goin' on . . .
Goin' on . . .

Chorus
I can't trust no more, you see,
'fraid your fishin's got the best of me.
There's trout and pike and largemouth bass.
I wish you'd shove them in the . . . grass.
I think there's somethin' fishy goin' on . . .
Somethin' fishy goin' on . . .
Yeah man, there's somethin' fishy goin' on.

As things turned out, that ain't the case.
From morn 'til night it's fish you chase.
There's lake and stream and river fish,
please quit this madness. "NOW!" I wish!
I think there's somethin' fishy goin' on . . .
Goin' on . . .

Repeat Chorus

We're bent and broke and downright lost,
you care not what your fishin's cost.
I wash your clothes in Pelly's Pond,
my nose tells me there's somethin' wrong.
I think there's somethin' fishy goin' on . . .
Goin' on . . .

REPEAT CHORUS

You say you're done once and for all,
next mornin' scales fall off your overalls.
Better things would come, a loan we'd float.
Ain't seen none yet 'cept your new boat.
I think there's somethin' fishy goin' on.
Goin' on.

*Illustration by Bob Hines, courtesy of the U.S.
Fish and Wildlife Service*

The First River Rat

It is the tag end of March and the southwest breeze and growing sun have dissolved most of the ice on Dark Slough. Here and there, thick, dark, honeycombed shore ice juts out a canoe length or so into the slough.

A critter swims along the edge of the shore ice, creating a V in the calm water. It swims purposefully—no dallying. It forges ahead until it comes to a tree lying in the water. The tree is a huge swamp white oak felled untold decades ago by a summer storm. Its roots lie on the bank and an ash tree grows on either side of its trunk. The ash acts as a hinge to hold the fallen oak in position while allowing the rest of the tree to float on the rising and falling waters of the Big River, like a slanted boat dock.

When the critter reaches the log, it grips the barkless wood with sharp, quarter-inch-long toenails and hauls itself out of the water. It shakes, spraying water droplets that sparkle in the sunshine. The critter's body is a foot long and covered with a dense coat of short brown fur. Inch-long mahogany guard hairs protrude from the coat the entire width and length of the back. The tail is three-quarters as long as the body, hairless, and the texture of soft leather. It is an inch wide and flat, but in the opposite way of the tail of its cousin the beaver. This tail is meant for use as a rudder.

Presently the critter stands upright on its hind feet, which are not webbed but rimmed with short, stiff hairs. It waddles forward, ducklike, a couple of feet farther up the

*Illustration by Charles Douglas, courtesy of
the Canadian Museum of Nature*

log. Then it stops. The small, pointed, bewhiskered nose twitches; tiny round ears stand erect; and its typically rodent, three-quarter-inch teeth click and clack together. The critter's dark, beady eyes look around alertly as the animal squats to deposit several drops of sticky liquid on the log.

This is a male muskrat. Only the males bear a pair of tip-of-your-thumb-sized musk glands on each side of the testes, which swell and fill with musk during breeding time. And this is a musk log used by one generation of rats after another, for as long as the log remains. The musk log is a social place, a community meeting center. Every muskrat that swims by it checks out the "posters" left by others. When two breeding-size males arrive at the same time, there is trouble along the Big River.

Today, the male on the musk log has company. A male of equal size sits hunched up on the other end of the musk log. His nose quivers as his tiny black eyes stare at the bold intruder. The two male rats eye one another for a long, tension-filled moment. Suddenly, they run toward each other to meet head-to-head in the middle of the slippery log. They stand on their hind legs, briefly grappling with each other. Then, almost faster than the eye can follow, the combatants roll and tumble end-over-end along the log, razor-sharp yellow teeth flashing in the sunlight and leaving a blood-spattered trail as they go. Like a jumping carp, the battling pair splashes loudly into the water. The little fury-filled critters swim as fast as they can; one is chasing the other. After a short pursuit, the "winner" returns to the musk log, crawls out of the water, and shakes himself, sending a mix of water and blood spraying into the air.

Each rat has inflicted several half-inch-long, half-moon-shaped cuts clean through the hide. But Nature's folks harbor great healing properties. After much licking, the wounds will heal, perhaps with a pus bag and a scar to show for it, but the tough little muskrats will live to swim another day.

After leaving a few pieces of scat, the winner feels his "calling card" is complete and slips into the Dark Slough waters. Sometime during the following night, Momma Muskrat visits the musk log. Pappa is there, and they breed, perhaps on the log or on a soft grass hummock along the bank. Now the male's work is finished, but Momma's is just beginning.

Generally, the Big River runs high during early spring breeding, due to northern snowmelt and springtime rains. When the female feels her babies grow, she excavates a foot-square den well above the waterline. The den connects to an underwater "front door" by way of a slanted tunnel. This way, if the water level rises during the first couple weeks, the kits, who are born hairless and helpless, will remain dry. If water does inundate the den, Momma will move the young, swimming with one baby at a time, held by the scruff of the neck, much like a mother cat would.

On a warm, sunny, mid-May day, the female gives birth to six young. She licks them dry and nurses them tenderly in the grass-lined den beneath an undercut bank where the grasses grow green and lush.

By the time spring dissolves into summer, the babies wear a coat of mousie-type fur that is beginning to turn from blue-gray to light tan. They are fortunate; the water has remained stable. Their momma tends to their every need and teaches them to swim. When they are weaned, she carries many mouthfuls of fresh green grass for them to eat. She swims back and forth again and again. Only one baby is lost and that to a snapping turtle. One minute, the little rat is swimming along; the next minute, it disappears beneath the water, never to be seen again. Once, a large boar raccoon succeeds in punching a small hole in the birthing den but thinks better of reaching in when Momma Rat appears at the hole, teeth chattering.

Of course, they contend with the daily dangers of mink and owls and the occasional water snake, but it has been so far so good for the little family. They still have much growing to do. Before fall, the kits will have young of their own to raise and their momma will have at least one more family as well.

With the first hard frost of autumn comes a new sense of urgency. Housebuilding! Some rats choose to winter in the many bank dens along Dark Slough, but most subdivide the tall stands of cattails and bulrushes into small parcels and erect dome-shaped huts. Each night as the wavering V's of migrating wildfowl cross the harvest moon, the muskrats are busy building. Some cut the frost-dried aquatic vegetation, others swim with it in their mouths, and still others hold tightly to their chests the vegetation and mud dredged from the slough bottom, as they shove and pile it in ever-increasing mounds. Building a hut is truly a family project.

Nobody goes to help their neighbors. When the main sleeping hut is finished, they work on the "kitchen," a feeder hut that is a replica of the main hut, only about one-fourth as large. Both huts have a front and back underwater entrance that come up onto a small, flat pad of dry vegetation. The muskrats clear an area of aquatic plants twenty-five feet around each hut, inadvertently making good "landing strips" for wildfowl and dipping and diving places for the birds to feed. The rats also create many floating "tables"—feed beds on which they sit and munch their meals.

Soon the white winds of winter blow strong from the north and the waters freeze over. The outsides of the mudded-up huts also freeze, making them airtight—a good R factor for insulation indeed. As the snow piles on the winter ice pack, the muskrats' world becomes dark and quiet. Only the creaking and cracking of the ice and the slurp of the water as a family member slides out the door can be heard. When a rat leaves the sleeping hut, it follows a trail in the muddy slough bottom—called a rat run—which is created by the muskrats' hind feet kicking to the side as they swim. Each rat in the family travels that trail, and before long, the rat run is six inches deep and easy to follow in the darkness. At least two rat runs lead from the sleeping hut to the tuber beds nearby. Here, the rats dig up the tubers, or roots, of arrowhead and cattails or water lotus and water lily.

When the rat has the root dug, it carries it in its mouth along another rat run to the feeder hut. Here, the muskrat sits on the small pad above the waterline, holds the root in its hand, and has its meal. When finished, the rat slides down the "plunge hole" into the water and retraces its path to the sleeping hut, where it crawls up to the "bedroom" pad and joins its four "roommates" for a nap. They pile on top of each other for warmth and security, like a litter of canine pups. During a day's time, they each take turns going out for breakfast, dinner, supper, and maybe a midnight snack as well. At times, when one gets up to leave, the others complain. There is a certain amount of discontent. But then you have that in the best of families.

One night during the late January thaw, a great danger comes to the sleeping hut. A large, hungry male mink comes to call. He digs through the hollow sleeping chamber. The hut's outside walls give way to the mink's efforts. In a flash, he enters. Before the rats can slide down the two plunge holes, the mink kills one with a savage bite to the throat. The rest of the little family escape.

The worst part is that the mink stays inside the hut to feed on the hapless rat's carcass, so the other muskrats cannot return to plug the hole with fresh mud and vegetation. After two days, the mink leaves, but the cold nighttime air has frozen solid the inside of the hut; there is no longer any way to enter the hut from below the ice. The remaining rats are homeless. They try to move in with their neighbors but are not accepted. There is only enough food and sleeping room for each hut's occupants. The homeless rats' only alternative is to swim for the bank of Dark Slough—a long ways under the ice.

The rats gather as much air into their lungs as they can and swim just beneath the ice pack, where they gain a fresh breath every few minutes from the occasional air pocket between the ice and the water's surface. As they travel, the rats come upon a scattering of "push-ups," places where vegetation has been pushed up through a hole in the ice. The push-ups were built by bank rats who are wintering in vacant birthing dens along the slough bank. When the bank rats swim from their dens to the tuber beds, they stop halfway there at a push-up. There is a fist-sized hole worn and chewed through the ice. The plant matter is piled a foot or more in height on the ice; this insulates the hole and allows them to stop for a breath of air on their long daily trips to the "grocery store."

The muskrats displaced by the marauding mink make good use of the push-up breathing holes before setting off on the final leg of their journey.

Finally, the rats reach the bank of Dark Slough. But they are not safe yet. They set to excavating a small den of their own. To reach unfrozen earth, the rats must dig an upward-slanted underwater tunnel to earth deep beneath the bank. Once the den is created, the rats are able to resume the business of daily living: sleeping, digging, swimming, eating, leaving scat in the water, and waiting—quietly, stoically—for spring to arrive. The danger has been thwarted, and, miraculously, the majority of the rats have survived.

As the long, cold winter wears on, the sun climbs higher, the days grow longer, and the winds begin to blow from the southeast. The ice pack above them becomes dark, rotten, and soft. Small open-water holes begin to appear. Alongside each, one or more muskrats take up seats, backs to the wind, munching on a snack, but they are always vigilant for the swish of a wing beat or a wavering sun shadow on the ice. The birds of prey are hungry, too.

Oh, how good it feels to the rat. Daylight, fresh air, soon-to-be fresh green shoots! Hallelujah! Free at last!

The Circle of Life has completed one turn. An ancient rhythm beats in the little heart of a most magnificent creature, the muskrat. With the coming of spring, all of their kind feel a call from the distant past:

"Come, my brothers and sisters. Once again you are free. Soak up the sun, hear the frogs and the birds, smell the Earth awakening, taste the fresh shoots. Travel, find adventure, seek your musk log and your mates for you must secure a future for yourself by being many."

It is no wonder those of us who love the Big River have made an icon of the muskrat by calling ourselves river rats. I know, however, that I can never measure up to the First River Rat.

Illustration by Bob Hines, courtesy of the U.S. Fish and Wildlife Service

Ever Been Lost?

Ever been lost? If your answer is no, I can think of three or four reasons you have experienced such good fortune while tooling about this world.

The most obvious way you could live your entire life without becoming lost is to stay put. Don't go nowhere. Stay in the same house, apartment, tent, or cabin where your parents raised you. If you do leave your home, you keep it in plain sight or at least in easy earshot. Probably not a whole lot of folks fall into this category, but I'm sure there are a few.

Then there are those of you who travel the same routes everywhere you go, whether you drive, walk, fly, or, for that matter, paddle a canoe. You always take the same way there and the same way back. Familiarity lends itself to security. However, I wonder what happened the first time you traveled that route. Could you have been lost?

I'm sure a number of you move about in this world strictly by commercial means: taxicabs, buses, airplanes, trains, guided walking tours, and such. This is an excellent way to avoid becoming lost insofar as fault is concerned. You have no responsibility here. If you do become lost, you lay the blame smack dab in the lap of the driver, pilot, engineer, or, if all else fails, at the feet of the commercial transportation company. You're along for the ride—period.

Somewhere on this Earth lurks the kind of human who possesses a wealth of orienteering knowledge. Couple that

*llustration by Bob Savannah, courtesy of the
U.S. Fish and Wildlife Service*

with an inability to make a simple judgment mistake and we have a real ball of fire. Whether you are navigating the skies or seas, traversing the Earth by highway, byway, back forty, or unadulterated wilderness, you are more than willing to share your expertise with anyone, anywhere, anytime. I have encountered experts like you at bait shops, sporting goods stores, and ski resorts. Even if you do not approach me with advice, you are easy to spot. You come standard with a lapel compass, a necklace compass, a belt compass, and one or more pocket compasses.

I once met a man who displayed all of the above on his person. He also sported a medium-sized compass mounted on the toe of each boot. He claimed this variation to be invaluable when traveling through rough terrain 'cause he didn't have to take his eyes off his feet to determine which direction he was headed. I forgot to ask him what value they were when tromping through deep snow or mud—guess I thought it irrelevant.

The other pieces of paraphernalia that identify the orienteering expert are maps. Maps stick out of—and at times fall from—every conceivable nook and cranny of your clothing, plus a goodly number are handheld. Road maps, topographical maps, contour maps, aerial maps, and at times a hand-drawn map or two. In my estimation, if I come across someone who carries all these compasses, maps, and associated survival gear in a briefcase—BEWARE. Briefcases have proven to be more than a little unwieldy when toted across certain types of landscapes.

You know what irks me about you expert orienteers? Most of you know how to use all those gadgets—and quite well at that!

What irks me even more is where in the Sam Hill are you when I'm floundering around in the middle of a six-thousand-acre swamp during a blinding snowstorm with a forty-below-zero windchill and I don't have a clue which way my camp is? Just ONE time during such a crisis, I'd like to have an expert like you step from behind a beaver lodge reading your compass, waving a map, and hollering, "Over here, my friend, your troubles are over!" Just one time. Just once!

Last, but certainly not least, are you folks who live in denial. You naysayers flatly deny ever having been lost in your lifetime. No way will I find a roadmap in your vehicle. You think anybody who can't find their way to their destination anywhere on the North American continent or indeed around the world is a brick short of a load. Who needs a trail guide? Good grief, you say. Aren't they all marked and wood-chipped? A blind pig could find its way around in this piddling little park! Compass? Map? Next thing we'll want you to pack a knife, matches, candy bars, and God knows what else! What are we, some kind of scaredy cats? Hell, man, you've been through country that'd make our hair stand on end. Only had the clothes on your back, and damn few of them at that, and you came out in fine shape. What are we anyway? Paranoid or something? Tell someone where you're going? You like your privacy! You go on to say: Whatever happened to travelin' by the sun, moss on the north side of the trees, reading the stars, following water downstream, and just plain using a sense of direction? This country's full of nothin' but a bunch of nitwit wimps! What's the world comin' to? The mountain men never carried all that kind of junk around with 'em, did they?

I believe your small, vocal, and at times influential group thrives and somehow gains inner strength from your denial.

Based on my personal experiences, I believe a few of you individuals could actually make the following scenario a reality, and perhaps already have:

A man with the "denial" mindset goes off into some wild, rugged country, ill-equipped and without telling somebody where he is going or when he expects to return. Several days later, the local game warden notices the man's four-wheel-drive truck parked on the side of a remote backwoods road. The warden radios the sheriff with the license plate number. The sheriff contacts the man's family; they have no idea what he is up to. Another day slips by before the officers become overly concerned and begin a search. For the next two days and nights, half of the county's able-bodied people, most all its hound dogs, and a fair number of aircraft scour the countryside for this person. On the eighth evening, he is found. When he staggers off the rescue helicopter at the local airport, newspaper reporters and TV cameras are there to get the story.

There he stands, a week's worth of stubble on his face, haggard, with cuts, bruises, and abrasions crisscrossing any exposed flesh. His shirt sleeves and pant legs are torn to tatters. What words of wisdom come out of his cracked, chapped, thirsty, hungry lips?

"Well, folks, it's good to be back, but I really wasn't lost you know," he whispers. "I just didn't know exactly where my truck was for awhile!" With a hoarse, strange little laugh, he limps off alongside a deputy, headed for the hospital.

Of course, plenty of us poor souls in this world answer the question "Ever been lost?" with a resounding, no-holds-barred, let-the-truth-be-known "YES!"

I don't suppose most of us "outdoor nerds" are especially proud of the fact that we've been lost a time or two or three when trekking about the countryside. In fact, some of us might try to salvage a little dignity by using sugarcoated terms to describe our "where am I?" experiences: "I was turned around." "I didn't know exactly where camp was." "I was disoriented." "I veered off course." "I got twisted up." "I couldn't find my way back."

What's wrong with a simple, little word like "lost"? Oh, mercy, Martha! There, I went ahead and said that awful four-letter word again—give me forty lashes with a wet noodle!

In some people's minds the word "lost" should never be used. Worse yet, I should never admit to having been lost at places like hunting lodges, fishing camps, trapping rendezvous, expeditionary conventions, or, for that matter, a genuine backyard campfire, lest some REAL outdoorsperson perceives me to be some bumbling survival-camp reject who can't find my way to my own kitchen unless raw onions are burnin' up on top of the stove.

Lost, you say? I've been lost more times than I've got fingers and toes to count 'em on. Can't say I'm proud of it; that's just the way things have been for me. I suppose I'll be lost again before I go to that great backwater swamp in the sky.

Illustration by Bob Savannah, courtesy of the U.S. Fish and Wildlife Service

Those Swamps You Call Home

She sat on a wooden bench, almost against the back wall of the nature center, during my one-hour talk on Nature and what it means to me. My gaze met hers perhaps a half-dozen times, as it did everyone else's in the room. But there was something different about her eyes; they didn't turn away or blink as readily as the others. It was as if she was studying me, as if she was wondering, *Does this guy really believe that critters are precious, that a simple life lived with Nature is the most rewarding of all?*

After my talk was over, she came to the front of the room along with seven or eight other folks, to shake hands and ask some questions about my lifestyle. When her turn came, she thrust out her hand and shook mine vigorously, looking me straight in the eye.

"Mr. Salwey," she said, "my name is Mary Beth. I go to college at Stevens Point."

"Call me Kenny," I said. "I guess I went to the school of hard knocks in the backwaters of the Mississippi."

She laughed. "Those swamps you call home sure sound interesting."

"Maybe you can come over to see the swamp sometime."

"Well, I . . . ," she stammered. "Yes!"

I wrote my name, address, and phone number down for her as I've done for many people at my talks. I figure the only way I can keep the joy I find in Nature is to give it away. We shook hands again, and she was gone. On the way home, I thought about how my wife Faye and I had discussed all the folks we'd given our address to and how few we ever hear from. A couple of months later, the phone rang.

"Hello," said the young lady on the other end. "This is Mary Beth from Stevens Point. Do you remember me?"

"I sure do, Mary Beth."

She went on to explain how she and a friend of hers would like to come to the river swamps for a weekend and write a story on our lifestyle. We agreed on Friday evening, the nineteenth of October, through the twenty-first. We'd meet at my little house in Buffalo City.

Mary Beth and her friend Vicky arrived late in the evening. Faye and I greeted them at the door, then piled their bags, backpacks, and other gear on the floor. Vicky and Mary Beth gave us some homemade bread and other goodies. Then we went up in the attic to look at my furs. Mary Beth was short, perky, and quick of step as she climbed the stairs. Vicky was tall and graceful. A study in contrasts.

The attic had low ceilings, a window on each end, and a single light bulb dangling from the ceiling. On all sides hung muskrats, mink, raccoon, and beavers drying on their stretchers. A pail full of fresh muskrat carcasses sat in the middle of the floor. From the rafters hung fleshing boards and knives of all sizes and shapes. The attic had a peculiar odor all its own—musky, greasy, strong. Yet when you sniff more than twice, you detect the catnip hanging in the far corner or maybe the ginseng drying on the screens. I watched their faces intently. Vicky's showed interest and curiosity. Mary Beth's registered disbelief, bordering on outrage.

They began asking questions: *How many critters do I kill in a year? In my lifetime? Why do I kill them? How long have I done this? How do I skin, flesh, and stretch them? What about the roots and herbs?* We sat down and talked. I tried to answer as best I could. I said I thought they'd understand the answers to these and many more questions much better tomorrow in the swamp.

Vicky and Mary Beth took to the floor in their bedrolls, Faye and I to our bed by the old woodstove.

"What do you think of those two young ladies?" Faye asked.

"I'll tell you more by Sunday night."

Five o'clock in the morning came fast. I walked to the living room door and hooted, "Who cooks for you, who cooks for you, who ah, who ah," like a barred owl. "It's daylight in the swamps, girls."

We had a good breakfast. Afterward, I noticed Vicky's jeans had some sizeable holes at the knees, after the fashion young folks like to wear nowadays. I mentioned to Vicky that the swamp was no damn park. She smiled good-naturedly and came out wearing a different pair of pants.

My Lab Joey and I got into my decrepit 1972 Pontiac. The two young ladies loaded their gear into their little car and followed us to the swamp shack, which sits on a high, wooded bank overlooking the Big Lake country.

Upon entering the shack, Mary Beth and Vicky slowly examined the contents. From the ceiling, hanging on strings, were turtle shells, herbs, pictures, tanned hides, grouse tails, and a multitude of other artifacts and utensils. Nails driven into the walls held the knives, forks, pots, pans, and clothes. On the east wall were four bunks with mattresses, pillows, and blankets. To the left of the door stood the wood box and a couple of old guns. A woodstove sat maybe six feet away. An oak plank table with matching benches stood between two windows facing Big Lake.

We went outside, where I showed them the outhouse, built from canvas and oaks in an A-frame shape over a hollow stump. We went back inside, where I supplied three ash walking sticks and fitted Vicky with a pair of rubber knee boots at least two sizes too big. Another pair of socks and felt insoles made them bearable.

"Mr. Salwey," Mary Beth said, "don't do anything different today 'cause we're here. Just pretend we're not here, and we'll just tag along."

Fat chance of that, I thought. *They'll probably be stuck in the mud within five minutes.* I smiled and said, "Well then, I reckon we'll go duck huntin' down on the east end of the Big Lake toward Crooked Slough."

The three of us, plus old Joey and all the gear, crossed the east end of Big Lake in a sixteen-foot canoe, then walked about a hundred yards to a willow point on Crooked Slough. There we sat in a little blind, watching the sun come up. It seemed to balance on the treetops, at the crest of the wooded hills. From time to time, gunshots echoed across the great river valley. To the south, somebody was blowing his lungs out on a duck call.

We talked about ducks, what they eat, how they live, and how they die. Why do I use a single-shot gun? Will there ever be a lot of waterfowl again? How was old Joey trained to be a swamp dog? We talked of herons, egrets, blue jays, and crows. The young ladies took pictures and brought out a tape recorder. We watched a brown creeper bird go up, down, and around a tree, and then wondered, did he always start from the top or the bottom? The hot tea and coffee from our bottles tasted good in the crisp autumn air.

We took up our walking sticks and walked south on the narrow strips of wooded land that separate the bogs and marshes. We stopped often to look at critter tracks, examine plants, and talk about leaves and trees. Now and again, we sat down and gazed over the swamp. We listened, smelled, and thought. We saw, felt, and touched the leaves, grass, and water. I told them this was what I call sauntering.

We sauntered for several hours and talked; always, we talked. About man's relationship to Nature, how you can tell what kind of duck it is by the way it flies, why the world is so consumed by greed. They taught me about the Tragedy of Commons and many others things they had studied in school. Always, old Joey was by our side. Once in awhile, a few ducks would be spotted, but none offered a good shot. Then it began to cloud over and look like rain, so we went back to the shack on Big Lake. Dried venison, homemade bread, and tea was our lunch. It began to rain, softly at first, then harder and steadier.

We lit a fire in the woodstove, then each took to a bunk to rest awhile. Mary Beth took the one directly above me, Vicky the other top bunk. Vicky, being taller, swung herself up and in with ease. Mary Beth had a little trouble, but she clawed and scratched until she made it, too. We all had a good laugh. Mary Beth had a good sense of humor and showed me she wasn't a quitter. Joey got on the lower bunk with me, curled up against my side, and went to sleep.

The rain pitter-pattered on the tin roof and the fire crackled. Lying there with my eyes closed, I smelled the familiar scents: wood smoke, herbs, and wet dog. Wait a minute. There was something else. My tired mind tried to identify it. Ah yes, a faint hint of perfume or maybe scented laundry soap, truly a foreign aroma in the old woodsman's shack. I chuckled to myself, *By golly, it smells good for a change*, then drifted off to sleep.

When I awoke, I stretched, swung my legs over old Joey, got up, and fired the stove. Vicky was still sleeping. Mary Beth was lying on her stomach, writing in a notebook. I walked to the window. A mist rose off the water. Across the river bottoms, maybe three miles away, the Minnesota bluffs stood tall and rugged. In the valleys, little patches of fog rose here and there. When the hills looked like that my dad always said, "The rabbits are cookin' coffee; it's gonna rain all day." And it usually did.

We spent all afternoon resting. When two of us were awake at the same time, we talked a little. Time meant nothing. Around suppertime, Faye came to the shack with grub. The young ladies asked what we were having.

"Fried potatoes and fried catfish," Faye answered.

We cooked supper on the woodstove, then sat up to the table. The young ladies had never eaten catfish before. After a little hesitancy, they pitched right in. Oh, how we ate!

After supper, Faye and the young ladies stayed in the shack, visiting like old friends, while Joey and I walked down to the dock to check the canoes. We stood on the end of the dock, listening and watching, as a seemingly endless string of blackbirds flew from the fields to their roost in the swamp. A fish rose just high enough to dimple the surface of the water. A hen mallard quacked loudly in the wild rice beds as the drakes softly chortled their feeding call. Finally, night drew its dark curtain over the swamp. I turned and walked up the bank to the shack.

"Let's go for a walk in the dark," Faye suggested, and off we went, following the dirt roads that crisscross the thirty acres of woods in back of the shack. Now night is dark no matter where you are, but you ain't seen dark 'til you've been in the swamp on a rainy night. We trudged along the dirt roads, taking half steps instead of full strides on the uneven terrain, bumping and jostling one another like a bunch of drunken sailors. No lights was the rule tonight. What fun is walking in the dark if you use a light? At one point we smelled a skunk.

"God, I hope Joey don't get ahold of that skunk," Faye said. "Oh yeah, we've had enough skunk-versus-dog episodes already to last me a lifetime."

We found our way to the ash-tree landing on Big Lake. After walking to the end of the dock, we stood still. The night was almost dead quiet. Just a whisper of a breeze drifted across Big Lake from the west. A great horned owl softly hooted from the top of a giant swamp white oak. We could almost feel the shiver of fear run through the little night critters, who knew only too well that the silent wings of death would claim one of them before morning. We turned and headed back toward the shack, laughing and talking like a group of schoolkids at recess.

The light from the two kerosene lamps cast eerie shadows across the ceiling and down the walls as we prepared for bed in the old shack. A huge fire-blackened kettle was filled with water and set on the woodstove to heat overnight, so we'd have warm water for washing in the morning. The lamps were blown out, and Mary Beth and Vicky took to the two top bunks, Faye to hers on the bottom, and Joey and I to what I affectionately called the Boar's Nest, a jumbled conglomeration of blankets, pillows, and quilts we straightened out once a month whether it needed it or not. Several times during the night, I rose to put more wood in the stove. Each time, I'd go outside for a few minutes. There's something about getting out of a warm bed and going outside to look at that snug little shack nestled on the banks of Big Lake with the wood smoke curling upward in the night air that does my heart good. The stars were out, and the harvest moon was about half full; tomorrow would be a nice day.

A flock of Canada geese flew low over the shack, calling in their wild, lonesome way. Back inside, I lay with my eyes closed, listening to their cries. Joey snored softly by my side. I opened my eyes, looked out the window, and saw the half light of dawn. I swung my feet to the floor and pulled on my bib overalls and an old wool shirt. Faye was next to rise, then the two young ladies. We busied ourselves filling the wood box, putting wood in the stove, and straightening the bunks. Faye took the big old washbasin off the wall, set it on the table, and poured it full of hot water from the kettle. Vicky and Mary Beth washed first, then I took my turn. I noticed their sidelong glances as I used the same water. There's only so much hot water when you heat it on the stove, and I didn't reckon their germs would kill me!

After a breakfast of leftover catfish, Faye left for home. Mary Beth and Vicky got their cameras, tape recorder, binoculars, and other gear together in their packs. Joey and I went down to the dock to ready the canoes. After we loaded our gear aboard the canoes, old Joey took her place in the bow. Mary Beth took the bow of the other, with Vicky in the stern. A couple shoves and we were off across Big Lake.

It was one of those mornings that cries out "autumn," the transition from summer to winter. The sky was a deep azure, fading to a light gray where it met the bluffs. The air was crisp and fresh, a delight to breathe. No wind and no clouds. Frost coated the cattails and the sides of the canoes. Where the sun hit the trees, water dripped from the branches as the frost melted. We paddled awhile, then stopped, leaving the canoes to travel their own course while we sat silently watching and listening.

"Why did we stop paddling, Kenny?" Vicky asked.

"This is called drifting," I answered. "I guess it's about like sauntering, only you're on the water." We watched a goshawk perched in a tree on the north end of Big Lake.

We followed Long Slough out the west side of Big Lake. Halfway to Long Lake, we stopped to examine a beaver house and feed bed. The young ladies sounded the entrance and exit holes out with their paddles, noting how the bottom mud was gorged out from the beavers swimming in and out of the house. The beavers had willow, dogwood, and popple branches piled in the water ahead of their house for winter feed. The beavers had plastered the house with mud to make it airtight, leaving a vent hole at the top for breathing. We talked about trapping beavers, how it is done, and how I had trapped on this same beaver colony for over fifteen years, taking a few each year and leaving the rest to tend the dams and carry on the colony.

On to Long Lake, then down Beaver Cut to the Tent Camp we went. The Tent Camp is a huge canvas, perhaps twenty-by-thirty feet, stretched over a framework of ash poles, with a wood floor resting on four barrels. The wooded bank where it sits is maybe five feet above the water. In times of high water, the tent floats but is held in the general area by four ropes. Inside the tent is an army cot, dry clothes packed in covered plastic pails, some cooking gear, and an old ice cooler to keep things from getting chewed by the field mice. We sat on the steps, made of two large chunks of oak, and talked of the long, hard winters trapping. What a real comfort the Tent Camp is when you fall through the ice and you're all alone.

We took up our walking sticks and headed south, past the wood duck pond, then over to the Button Brush Slough. Hardwood trees and small lakes and ponds are the hallmark of this part of the swamp. Old Joey usually took the lead, checking all her familiar points of interest along the way. She's traveled this swamp for many years in all kinds of weather and in every season. Now, at twelve years of age, she's a real swamp dog—scarred and tough, yet gentle and loving. We sat by some button brush looking at the little, round seedpods that give them their name, and we talked of the times I followed Joey back to camp in a heavy fog and why I feel my dog is my best friend.

On the east side of Schultz's Pond we sat on an old deadfall watching the sparkling blue water ripple in the gathering breeze. We talked of Mary Beth's home and family in Florida, Vicky's life in eastern Wisconsin, and my ancestors—Frenchmen who had hunted and gathered like myself. We wondered if Nature would be able to heal itself from the wounds man has inflicted upon it. Or, would we destroy Nature and ourselves as well? I asked Vicky if she was cold.

"Only my hands and one cheek," she said, gesturing to the log she sat sideways on. Mary Beth thought perhaps Vicky should turn the other cheek! We laughed, then started for the Big Marsh Shack, following an ancient deer trail through the timber.

Just short of the Marsh Shack, we met two duck hunters returning from the morning's hunt. They wore chest waders and Gore-Tex hunting coats. Their guns were oiled and varnished semiautomatics. Duck calls and dog whistles hung from lanyards about their necks. Old Joey circled their two black Labs, stiff-legged with hackles raised as if to say, *Hey, pals, this is my territory.*

Later, the young ladies asked me why I didn't use fancy equipment for hunting. I told them I didn't reckon I needed it just to get a duck or two now and then for the oven, but to each his own, I guess. Ten minutes later, we were at the Marsh Shack.

The Marsh Shack is a wood-frame building about sixteen feet square, covered with tar paper on all sides plus the roof. Rows of barrels sit beneath the floor so it floats high and dry in times of high water. One window faces the open marsh to the west, the other the south marsh, while the back of the shack nestles against the woods. Inside is a woodstove, a row of stacked wood, four bunks, a table and chairs, and some small cupboards. We sat by the table and talked of how this shack had withstood forty years of weather and high-water floods, and how a shack takes on a character all its own, almost a spirit you can feel when you're sitting there. The early fall days spent sitting on the front steps, half-asleep in the warm afternoon sun. The January days when you're inside, woodstove a cookin', wind howling, snow blowing with just those thin walls between you and winter's fury. We left the shack, heading north along the Tent Camp Slough.

The sun had dried the frozen leaves to the consistency of fresh cornflakes. They cracked and crunched under our feet as we walked single file through the lowland forest. Where the slough forks stands an ancient swamp white oak looking down from the bank on a deadfall in the water. In fall, the wood ducks love to gather acorns at the base of the old oak, then waddle down to the water and sun themselves on the deadfall. Their white bellies lined the log like a bunch of turtles in the summer. The wood ducks flushed like a covey of quail as we approached. We sat down under the giant oak. I told the ladies how old Spook, my swamp dog before Joey, and I had spent our last day in the swamp together right on this very spot. We talked of dogs and friends and special places, then continued on along the east bank of the slough till we reached our canoes by the big beaver dam.

We loaded our gear, then paddled leisurely back the way we had come, to the Big Lake Shack. The ladies loaded up their car, double-checked the shack, and it was time to say goodbye. I shook their hands, they thanked me graciously,

I said the last two days were entirely my pleasure, and they were off. Joey and I stood by the shack door waving as they drove away. The brake lights of Mary Beth's little car came on, and they backed down the dirt road toward us. The ladies got out. Each gave me a big hug, and we shook hands again. They said something about a handshake not being enough to show their appreciation for the tour of the swamp, and to tell Faye thanks a million. We said goodbye, and they were gone.

Old Joey and I went down to the dock. I tipped the canoes over against a yellow birch, put a boat cushion on a five-gallon pail on the dock, and sat down. A few ducks traded calls back and forth across the swamp as dusk began to set in. Old Joey lay on the grass bank, ears perked, sniffing the evening air. A stiff breeze blew from the northwest, making a long blade of dry marsh grass undulate back and forth. How long I watched that blade of grass I do not know, but I know a lot of thoughts crossed my mind.

I felt as if I had just said goodbye to a couple of dear friends, even though I had only known the ladies for a couple of days. I was not used to sharing my thoughts and feelings, being alone the way I am most of the time. Maybe it was the way Mary Beth smiled with that little space between her front teeth and those piercing, inquisitive eyes that said, *You can trust me. All I want to do is learn about Nature's ways. Maybe I don't agree entirely with your lifestyle, but now at least I know why you live the way you do.* I thought of the morning before when I saw Mary Beth was out of coffee for her thermos. I volunteered to make some and noticed she didn't drink it too heartily. Later, I tasted some. God, it was awful: too thick to drink and too thin to chew. But she never said a word. I looked up across Big Lake and smiled.

Maybe it was Vicky's way of being gentle and innocent on the one hand, yet hard and tough on the other. I thought of her paddling hard through the wild rice, pulling the canoe up the bank, and falling flat on her back, only to get right up and smile. Yes, I guess it was all those things that made those ladies special, but I think the one thing that drew us together most was the fact that we found a common bond. We were of a kindred spirit; we all loved Nature. I, of course, had grown up surrounded by Nature and its critters. This sometimes leads one to take Nature for granted. By traveling the swamps together, Vicky and Mary Beth had given me a precious gift—the chance to see Nature through their eyes in all its newness, freshness, and wonder. For that, I shall always be grateful.

The hoot of an owl brought me back to reality. I stood on the bank of Big Lake watching darkness come once again to my beloved swamp, and I knew not just myself but Nature as well was much richer for having met and known those two young ladies.

The River Rolls Along

It knows no sense of time,
no clock tickin' off the days,
just travels on its weary way,
tellin' a story through this rhyme.

Chorus
The River rolls along
while we sing our song.
It's an old-time song
'bout days long gone.
The River rolls along.

There's been plenty of sand and mud
squeezed between my toes.
An old wood boat nobody rows
sunk long ago in a springtime flood.

An old cane fishin' pole
standin' 'longside a willow tree
ain't used no more, it's plain to see.
New gear now at the fishin' hole.

Bull frogs are a croakin',
catfish sometimes jumpin',

barges full of somethin',
old riverboat stacks are smokin'.

Winding past the cottonwood
tree that hums a lullaby
for you and me—just you and I.
Cares slip away and that feels good.

No one knows when it was found.
Some say the River ends
around its last bend.
That ain't so cause the
river's round.

*llustration by Bob Hines, courtesy of the
U.S. Fish and Wildlife Service*

Kickin' Skunk Cabbage

The old wagon creaked and the horses' harnesses squeaked as Pa and I crossed the lowland-meadow cow pasture. The pasture lay downhill of the family farmstead, which sat on a small hill overlooking the rugged hill country of the Mississippi River Valley.

Pa and I sat side by side. Pa held the long leather guide straps loosely in his work-worn hands. There wasn't much need to steer the team of horses 'cause they knew where we were going. And so did I! As we rolled and bumped through the dips and gullies, I wished we could go faster. This was fencing day. I was so excited I could hardly stand it. It was the spring of my eighth year, and Pa had said I could help him check and fix the cow pasture fences. Boy, who knew what I would see today!

"Whoa," Pa finally called out long and slow. Our team, Daisy and Sally, stopped at the fence. Pa handed me the long leather straps. "Stay where you are, son." He stepped off the wagon, put a wood-handled hammer in the cloth loop on his bib overalls, a handful of metal staples in his front pocket, and big metal fencing pliers in his hip pocket. He turned to me. "I'm gonna start walking along the fence. When I raise my arm, you drive the wagon to where I'm at, okay?"

"Sure will, Pa," I returned.

Pa walked along the fence. He took hold of the top of every oak fence post, gave it a good sharp pull, checked the

Illustration by Bob Savannah, courtesy of the U.S. Fish and Wildlife Service

barbed wire for tightness, and kept on walking. Once in a while, he drove a staple into the post to hold the wire tighter. About eight or ten posts down the line, he raised his arm.

"Gid up there," I said. The horses leaned into their harnesses and the wagon lurched ahead. Daisy and Sally plodded toward Pa. When the wagon came alongside Pa, the horses stopped. I hollered a long, slow "Whoa" anyway.

Pa said the post was rotted. It hung in place, held upright by the three barbed wires. I got down from the wagon to help Pa unload a new post. He took a post hole digger and began to dig a new hole. We put the post in the hole, he shoveled dirt in around it, and I tamped the fresh ground tight around the post with a tamping pole, which was a peeled ash sapling about six feet long. We nailed the wires on the new fence post, then took the wires off the old one and put it in the wagon. We'd cut the old fence posts up for firewood back at the farm.

So it went for the next few hours. The horses and I followed Pa along the fence line. At times, while I waited for the signal to go forward, I dreamed of "really" driving the horses in the fields, to make hay or plant corn. By now I realized that the team would stop wherever Pa was standing. I still hollered a long slow "Whoa" anyway, 'cause it felt so good to be grown-up.

While I waited for my signal from Pa, I watched the horses switch their long brown tails back and forth, to guard against the flies, and snort and mutter messages to each other. Once, I saw a blue flash from the corner of my eye. On top of a fence post sat a bluebird. In the bright spring sunshine, it sang a lovely song for me. Then it flew to a nearby post and disappeared into a hole. *A nest, I'll bet*, I thought. *Yup, a bluebird nest.* I looked up just in time to see Pa's arm raised. The team, the wagon, and I moved ahead. As we approached, I noticed Pa hold his fingers to his mouth. The horses stopped; I remained quiet.

"Git the rifle," Pa whispered. I crawled to the back of the wagon where a single-shot .22 caliber rifle lay behind a pile of fence posts. I snatched it up and took it to Pa. He handed me a bullet. "There's some striped gopher holes in yonder banks," he said softly. "Saw one go in there when I walked up." He pointed to the holes a short distance away.

I got off the wagon, carefully loaded the rifle, leaned against a fence post, and cocked the rifle. Pa let out a sharp whistle. Nothing happened. Again, he whistled. This time a plump little gopher came out of a hole, sat up on his haunches, and looked at us. I aimed the rifle and fired. With the crack of the bullet, the gopher jumped back down the hole.

Pa shook his head. "Gotta take a finer aim next time." As I put the rifle back into the wagon, I thought of the five-cent bounty I'd lost. There went my candy bar down that hole in the ground.

Pa joined me in the wagon. He drove the team down a long slope and pulled up under a large bur oak next to the Yeager Valley Crick, which meandered through the cow pasture meadow like a great snake.

Where the fence line crossed the crick there was big trouble. The rain-swollen crick had torn out the fence earlier in the spring. We would have to rebuild the fence. I carried the hammer, staples, and fencing plier. Pa took fence posts and barbed wire. Daisy and Sally rested in the shade of the bur oak.

We were halfway to the fence line when I noticed some dark green, broad leaves jutting up from the cool, moist ground. I gave them a kick and the pieces flew. A few more steps, some more leaves. I kicked them again and watched the pieces fly. A third time, I spotted those big green leaves ahead of me. This time I backed up, took a few quick steps, and gave those leaves a really good, hard kick. *Kawap*. The pieces sailed in the air. One of the larger leaf chunks cartwheeled ahead of me. I watched it go high in the air and then, as if in slow motion, begin to fall. *Oh no, it won't, will it? Oh yes, it did!*

Ka-plop. The leaf chunk hit the back of Pa's neck. A chunk of mud must have been attached to that bright green leaf 'cause it stuck to Pa's neck like a poultice. Slowly Pa's fingers groped behind his neck. They clamped on the leaf, and he brought it around to look long and hard at the mud-slathered object that had stuck to him. He turned to me and stuck one big thick finger out, crooked it, and signaled me to come.

Pa was not a happy camper. I knew he didn't want a tool that I carried. My steps were as short and slow as I could make them.

When I got there, I stood alongside him looking down at my feet. I noticed the toe of a rubber boot working its way back and forth in the crick-bank mud. I focused on that toe. I watched it as though it was someone else's toe doing the digging.

Pa held the mud-stained, bright green leaf in front of me. "How'd this thing come to end up on the back of my neck?"

"I guess I was kickin' at them leaves and a piece flew up in the air and hit ya."

"What was you kickin' at 'em for?"

My reply came almost in a whisper: "Oh, I don't know. Guess it was just something to do."

There was a long, drawn-out silence. I shifted my attention from my nervous toe to a robin singing its springtime song on a tree branch across the crick. I hoped Pa would take his eyes off me to look at the robin as well, but he didn't.

Finally, he said, "Take a good look at this leaf. It's the first green thing we've seen since early last fall. Kinda pretty, ain't it?" Without waiting for my answer, he went on. "Feel of it, boy," he ordered.

I did so gingerly.

"Feel them little ruffles and what seems like small veins in there?"

"Yup, I do, Pa. Kinda like the leaves on Ma's garden cabbage."

For the first time since I'd come over by him, I looked at Pa. A small grin creased his lips. "Now crush a bit of this leaf between your fingers and smell of it."

I hesitated.

"Go on. It ain't gonna hurt you none."

I did as he asked. "Wow, it stinks like a skunk!" I cried.

Pa laughed. "Yup, this plant looks and feels like cabbage and it smells like a skunk. That's why it's called skunk cabbage. You see, Kenny, this is one of the very first green things that pokes its head from the earth in the spring. It's all curled up in the beginning like a sort of cone. Each day the leaves unfurl a little more till they look like they do now—bright green and broad. It's a sure sign of spring. Kinda nice to see after a long hard winter, wouldn't you say?"

I nodded.

He went on. "Some of the old-timers used the leaves and roots for remedies of one sort or another. Ain't no other plant that smells like it either. All things belong to the great Circle of Life. Each one has its own special place and that includes us."

He stopped and looked into my face. His dark eyes seemed to pierce clean through me. "That's why we don't kill something just to watch it die, to waste it or ruin it for nothing, do we now?"

"No, we don't, Pa."

Pa wasn't finished yet. "If I ever ketch you doing something like you done today, you'll be running through the cow pasture hollering there's a man after you. Understand?"

I allowed as how I understood perfectly.

* * *

The rest of that spring afternoon was spent fixing fence; however, my mind wasn't on it. I had a brand-new interest: skunk cabbage! Each time I'd come across a broad, bright green leaf, I would snip off a little corner, rub it between my fingers, smell of it, and run to Pa.

"This is skunk cabbage, ain't it?" I'd ask.

"Yup," he'd say, "that's what it is for sure."

That evening, my older brother Gerry, Ma, Pa, and I gathered around the supper table. Suddenly, Ma raised her nose to the air and declared, "Something stinks and it sure ain't the supper I've made. Smells like skunk in here. Did one of you guys or one of the dogs get too close to a skunk today?"

We shook our heads no. I reached into my pocket and produced a small piece of bright green leaf, rubbed it between my fingers, and held it out toward Ma. With a certain amount of pride, I explained what had happened down by the crick that afternoon. Ma was not impressed. No sense of awe or curiosity or enjoyment at all.

She sputtered explicit instructions as to what I was to do next. "You get that piece of leaf out of this kitchen. Take it outside. And I don't mean later tonight or tomorrow. I mean right this minute. And when you come back in you wash your hands with that bar of Lye soap and more than once. You hear me?"

I headed for the door without answering. After washing, I settled back at my place by the table. While eating, I glanced up at Pa. His eye closed in a long, slow wink.

This little setback did not deter me from seeking my newly found friend, the skunk cabbage plant, one least bit. In fact, my interest in it increased with each passing day—not to the point of obsession, but I did dream of it at night and look for it every spare moment of the day.

So it naturally followed that during my walks to the little wood-framed Anchorage schoolhouse about a mile from home, I would look for skunk cabbage along the way. I soon realized that by following the road I would find nothing. There was no running water, and though the soil was good for growing crops, not one broad, bright green leaf could be seen. Several days passed without a single find. This was awful.

I asked Pa whether he thought any skunk cabbage would be growing along the Waumandee Crick. He thought there should be some and that the only way I'd ever find out was to go and look for myself.

Now the Waumandee Crick wove back and forth through a long wooded valley not more than a half-mile south of our little farm. If I went over there and followed it upstream, I'd end up right in back of the schoolhouse. Mighty handy situation, to my way of thinking.

The next morning, I was up at the crack of dawn. After I gobbled down breakfast, I grabbed my little burlap shoulder bag and my walking stick and I headed through our "night pasture" toward the Waumandee Crick. It was the first time in my life I started for school early.

It was a lovely spring morning. The bright yellow sun

balanced on the treetops of the eastern hills. As I walked through the lowland meadows, a small covey of bobwhite quail flushed ahead of me. I stopped for a few moments to listen to the quail give their namesake call—*bobwhite, bobwhite*—in their regrouping effort. A meadowlark whistled its long clear notes from atop an old wooden fence post. A cottonwood tree stood on a small rise in the meadow. From its branches, a robin greeted the rising sun. Its lovely song drifted in long, lilting verses on the warm springtime breeze.

A feeling that all was right with the world welled up in me. I went forward with a spring in my step and joy in my heart.

I came to a three-strand barbed-wire line fence at the edge of a small wooded hollow. This was where Pa's land ended and our neighbors Lester and Adeline Planks's land began. I crossed between two strands of barbed wire carefully so as to not tear my bib overalls. I thought, *Boy, this going to school is a real pain. If it was any other day, I could crawl underneath the fence, but I don't want to get my overalls dirty for school today.*

As I passed through the small wooded lowland hollow, a couple of gray squirrels and a fox squirrel ran and climbed up various bur oaks. Mmm—I'd have to remember this. Might get one for supper some day next fall.

At the end of a field, near the edge of the woods, there lay several small brush piles where Lester had trimmed trees. I walked quietly to the first one and jumped on the brush. Nothing happened. I used the same approach on the second pile of brush. Two cottontail rabbits busted out from underneath the brush. The third brush pile yielded one more cottontail. I watched its little round puff of a white tail bob up and down as the rabbit bounded away through the prickly ash thickets. Wow, I'd have to check out these brush piles come next winter for sure.

In a short while I reached the east bank of the Waumandee Crick. The crick was twenty to thirty feet wide at most places. Today, the water ran low and clear. The snowmelt water had already passed and the heavy rains of late spring had not yet come. I gazed into the water and wondered where it was coming from, where it was going, and what it would see along the way. I followed the crick upstream. Now my search for skunk cabbage began in earnest.

After some distance I came to a sharp bend in the crick where I heard what sounded like water splashing. I walked carefully to the edge of the bank. There I found a large log with the butt end wedged under the bank. The small end of the log lay midstream, where the current was strongest. This caused the end of the log to rise out of the water for a second or so. Then it submerged again with a small splash. I stood mesmerized by the gurgling and splashing of the smooth, bark-free log as it bobbed to the rhythm of the happy crick. It was like a dance performed to an endless crick-bed song.

Suddenly I became aware of a long brown critter swimming along the opposite bank. It nervously investigated every tree root and hole at the water's edge. The critter's slender body moved with ease and grace. The guard hairs on its back shone in the sun-dappled water. *A mink! It's a mink!* I had only seen one mink before in my life when I was trout fishing the previous summer; however, I knew this critter was no doubt a mink. Holy moly, what an adventure this day was!

The little white schoolhouse was not too far in the distance when I came to a trickle of water bubbling out of the ground at the base of a large basswood tree. It was a genuine hill country spring, pure and clear as gin from a bottle. No self-respecting hill country lad would come upon a spring without taking a drink. I put one knee down on my gunnysack bag, cupped my hands together, and dipped out some water. It tasted cold and sweet.

The earth along the spring was black and rich and wet. It looked like good ground for skunk cabbage so I followed the spring toward the crick. Before long, the land became swampy and I hopped and jumped from one grassy hummock to another to stay out of that black, slimy mud. I stopped for a moment to catch my balance and there they were right at my feet—big, broad, bright green leaves. I looked up. They were all around me. It was breathtaking, a virtual field of skunk cabbage. The mother lode of all cabbage patches had been discovered by little old me.

I stood there awestruck. Then I threw caution to the wind and plunged in up to my knees in the rich black mud. I plucked small pieces of leaves and put them in my bag as fast as I could. When the school bell rang, my senses began to return. In this instance, "saved by the bell" was more than just another cute phrase. Who knows what would have become of me had that bell not rung when it did? I stopped to listen and it rang again. Quickly, I wallowed out of the patch to find solid footing on higher ground. I looked down at my pant legs and shoes. What a sorry mess!

I followed the crick upstream to a spot about one quarter of a mile directly in back of the schoolhouse. Here, an old wooden-plank bridge spanned the Waumandee Crick. It was used by a farmer, Walter Mosiman, to get his machinery to the land on the other side of the crick. Just upstream from the bridge a small sandbar jutted out a third of the way into the crick. I waded out until I was up to my knees in water. Then I washed my pant legs and shoes off as best I could.

After climbing out of the crick, I wrung the water from my clothes. As I was standing there enjoying the warmth of the sun, a red-winged blackbird perched on the edge of the bridge. *Konk-ah-ree*, it called out to me. It sounded like "come to me," so that's what I did. The bird moved to a crick-side willow and stared at me.

I lay down on my belly on the sun-warmed planks, cupped my hands around my face, and peered into the four or five feet of water that swirled and eddied beneath the bridge. What was that? Fish! At least three or four good-sized fish contentedly finned away the morning in the quiet pool below me. Wouldn't that just be the case now? Here I am late for school already and there are nice fat fish here just waiting to be caught for supper. School, school, and more school. Bah humbug!

I gathered myself up and headed across Walter Mosiman's cow pasture, up a steep one-hundred-foot wooded knoll, then kitty-corner across an open field at a quick pace to the schoolhouse. I took the steps two at a time. The door opened into a small entryway where I stashed my bag of skunk cabbage leaves under my jacket. I propped the walking stick in a corner. I stood there for a moment to catch my breath and steady my nerves. Then I tiptoed to the back of the classroom and eased myself into my little wooden desk.

The teacher, Mrs. Wendland, was working on some papers at her desk. My butt had hardly touched the chair when her head snapped up. This woman had the hearing capacity of a red fox listening for mice in an alfalfa field during a windstorm. She stared at me. She said one word:

"Kenneth."

"Yes, Mrs. Wendland," I answered in a small, soft voice.

She looked at the big clock on the wall. "Seems like you are one hour and forty-one minutes late for school again today. Am I not correct?"

There were two things that I didn't care for in her statement/question. The first was how she emphasized the word "again." The second was the way she said "am I not correct." I never knew how to answer when she said that, but I took a stab at it. "Yes, Mrs. Wendland," I said in an even smaller, softer voice.

By now, twenty-one pairs of ears were fine-tuned to every sound inside those schoolhouse walls. It was dead quiet except for the rather one-sided conversation between me and Mrs. Wendland.

"Kenneth, will you please come to the front of the room?"

Slowly, I stood up and walked down the row toward Mrs. Wendland. She stood up in front of the blackboard, which took up the better share of the front wall. As I walked, a weird cadence slapped out as my wet pant legs rubbed together. I knew twenty-one sets of eyeballs were glued to my every move. Some girl giggled. I felt like I was onstage in the spotlight at the Metropolitan Opera. Crawling into a hole would have been a welcome relief; however, there were none handy.

When I reached the teacher, she told me to take up a piece of chalk and print my name in large letters on the blackboard. I did so. Then she said to print the word tardy next to my name. I looked at her sideways.

"T-A-R-D-Y," her coaching went. It was the one word I should have known how to spell, but I didn't. Next, she told me to write April 3, 1951, on the board. When I completed my task, Mrs. Wendland informed me that during the noon hour, while the other children played, I was to go to the outdoor hand pump, pump a pail of fresh drinking water, and bring it inside. Also, I would be required to stay after school to give the blackboard a thorough washing and to dust the erasers.

She sent me back to my desk to print these words one hundred times: "KENNY WILL NOT BE TARDY AGAIN."

Pa always said, "Something good comes from everything that happens to you." I guess, in this case, at least I learned to spell "tardy."

An hour later, Mrs. Wendland left the schoolhouse to go to the main-road mailbox for her daily mail-collecting trip. As soon as she left, a friend of mine, Roger Harm, turned at his desk and hollered, "What was you doing this morning, Kenny?"

"Digging skunk cabbage," I hollered back.

"Skunk cabbage—what's that?" he asked.

"I'll show you." I made a dash for my bag in the entryway. I was back in a flash. I dumped my sack full of broad, bright green pieces of leaves on the floor. Twenty-one kids, in grades one through eight, gathered around me. I proudly crushed a few pieces and handed them to some of the boys.

"Smell 'em," I said.

They did so. "Waaah, does that stuff stink!" cried Roger.

"Yowser, it's just as bad as a skunk," moaned Delmar Plank.

"It would gag a maggot!" screamed Ardell Hanson.

The boys began pushing and shoving to get at a piece of a leaf for themselves. Meanwhile, the girls huddled together on the other side of the room. They looked like a flock of sheep facing a pack of crazed wolves. The girls' eyes were wide with expectant terror. They knew the mindset of the boys in a situation like this. They had been through it before with snowballs and mud pies and garter snakes. Pauline Bade made a valiant effort to stand her ground, but the sight of Roger Harm running toward her, laughing hysterically, crushed leaf in his outstretched hand, sent poor Pauline scurrying for the entryway door.

That's when total mayhem broke loose. Boys chased girls like dogs after cats. Kids ran every which way. Girls hid under coats. Some climbed on top of tables and desks. There was screaming, crying, and whining from both boys and girls. A couple girls stopped and turned to face their antagonists, stuck out their tongues, and hissed. As in most dog-cat chases, this dumbfounded the boy. The only safe haven seemed to be the girls' toilet, where most of the girls ended up, with the boys pounding on the door.

Just then Mrs. Wendland came through the door. She seemed a bit riled up. Her face turned the color of a ripe tomato. Fire lit her eyes.

"Everyone take your seats right now!" she shouted. "What's going on in here?"

One of the girls piped up: "Kenny brought a bag of skunk cabbage in here, and the boys were chasing us with it."

Mrs. Wendland moved a trampled leaf on the floor with her toe, reached down, picked it up, and gingerly sniffed it. She uttered one sound—"Whew"—and dropped it like a hot potato.

She stared hard at me. "So you're the culprit behind this awful mess."

I looked down at my shoes and counted the lace holes in the leather.

"Kenny, you clean up every scrap of this stuff, take it outside, and get rid of it permanently. Then you go into the washroom and scrub yourself clean as a whistle. The rest of you boys better do the same. One at a time, you hear me?"

When we were all through scrubbing ourselves, she had each of us hold out our hands and she came around to give us the sniff test. And I received another heavy workload to do after school for the next week or so.

So it was that I began to understand the great difference between boys and girls and men and women. It went beyond the obvious physical differences and manner of dress. The skunk cabbage proved, beyond a shadow of a doubt, the yawning gap in the attitudes and values between the sexes when it came to certain things in the great Circle of Life.

This was a valuable lesson to have learned and one that I have had ample opportunity to test over the course of the past fifty-four years.

Each year, when the Canada geese come north to nest and the red-winged blackbird tells of the coming of spring, when the robin heralds the dawn and the Earth sends its pungent odor of rebirth to waft on a warm breeze, I seek those broad, bright green leaves and I am grateful for the day so long ago when Pa caught me kickin' skunk cabbage.

*Illustration by
Tom Kelley,
courtesy of the
U.S. Fish and
Wildlife Service*

A Boy, a Grampa, a Swamp

Nobody loves the Mississippi backwater swamps, its marshes and duck-hunting, more than my longtime friend Dick Fleming, so it was only natural that he wanted to share this place with his grandson Mike, who was about seven or eight years old.

Dick and I agreed that the best time for Mike's introduction to the watery, muddy world of the swamp was early spring, when the ducks and geese were returning, the temperatures were mild, and enough safe ice remained for easy traveling. No slogging and sloshing through that black, boot-sucking, Mississippi mud for us!

Our long-awaited rendezvous at Big Lake Shack came on a Saturday morning in late March. Dick stepped from the truck impeccably dressed in L.L.Bean– and Eddie Bauer–type outdoor clothes. Mike hopped out beside his grandfather, wearing a stocking cap, flannel shirt, blue jeans, and new rubber-soled Sorrels. We shook hands heartily, took up our walking sticks, and set off into the swamp.

We traveled easily and comfortably, the way good friends will, stopping often to chat about past times spent in that wild and wonderful place. River birch, silver maples, and swamp white oak trees were identified, along with cattails, bull rushes, and button brush.

Mike was all eyes and ears, saying little except for "Grampa Dick, this is exciting!" or "Boy, we're sure going far into the swamp, ain't we, Grampa Dick?"

We visited familiar hunting spots like Button Brush Pond, Horseshoe Lake, and finally Maple Tree Pond, where we sat on an old log to lunch a bit. While we palavered back and forth, a pair of geese circled a patch of open water toward the west side of the pond.

"What kind of geese are they, Grampa?" Mike asked.

"They're Canada geese, Mike," Dick whispered. "If we're quiet, they might land."

We hunkered down and, sure enough, the geese landed with a swish about seventy yards from us, swam round a bit, climbed out on the ice, and stood there surveying their possible nesting site.

"Grampa, think I could get a picture of 'em?" Mike asked in a hushed voice.

"Don't see why not. Sneak up on 'em a little, real slow. Be careful on the ice. Stay away from those dark spots—they're weak."

Mike began his stalk, slowly, from tree to tree, then from one clump of dead grass to another, little camera hanging from his neck as he crouched. Dick and I glanced at each other, winked and smiled knowingly, both holding our breath, hoping the boy would get his picture. After all, this was his first "hunt." We wished it to be one he'd never forget. When we looked back toward Mike, we realized he was getting too close to the open water. His feet weren't far from black honeycombed ice. The geese seemed frozen, as if posing.

Mike was aiming his camera when he went down. Water and mud sprayed upward and Mike floundered about, then turned and looked at us as if to say, *Now what do I do?*

We hurried over and pulled Mike from the mire. That poor boy was a grimy, slippery, slimy mess if there ever was one! Water and mud oozed out of every pocket, down his pant legs, and out of the top of his boots. The three of us sat down on our "lunch log" with Mike in the middle. Dick and I wrung out Mike's pant legs, pulled off his boots, and replaced his socks with a spare pair. After a fair amount of squeezing and twisting, some of the gunk came off his boots and we put them back on him. Mike shivered, saying nothing.

"It ain't so bad, Mike," Dick said. "We'll be back to Big Lake Shack in no time at all." Dick and I had taken enough dunkings and mud baths in our time to know how cold and miserable one feels after such an experience.

But Mike's first words were, "Did you see how big them geese were? Sure were pretty, sure were pretty."

"Ready to head back now, Mike?" Dick asked. "Are you cold?"

"No, I ain't cold, Grampa. I thought Kenny was going to show us his Marsh Shack today!"

I looked at Dick, we raised our eyebrows, shrugged our shoulders, and started off toward the Marsh Shack country. Along the way, Mike inspected deer tracks, raccoon dropping, and hollow trees as if he were on a Sunday afternoon stroll through the park—no hurrying, no whining, no complaining, just good old downright enjoyment of the day.

At the shack, we encouraged Mike to put on some of my dry clothes and we thought maybe we should light a fire in the wood-burning stove. Mike said he was just fine and wanted to go see the Grandmother Tree, and away we went. At the site of my old Tent Camp, he dug through some old weathered bones he found beside a mound of dirt by my critter pit. We checked out a beaver dam, looked at some red dogwood, and talked of how good it was to hear the calls of the wood duck and the red-winged blackbirds. Finally, the three of us stood beside my beloved old Grandmother Tree, where I told the story of how her huge, dead, hollowed-out trunk had sheltered me and my dog on an overnight stay during a springtime snowstorm.

Mike crawled inside the Grandmother Tree to lay down, wet and soggy, just as I had been some twenty-odd years before, to be comforted and quieted in her bosom. A short time later we made our way back to Big Lake Shack, where I presented Mike with a well-worn snapping-turtle shell. I pointed out the thirteen parts to its shell, and he asked me how this came to be. I explained that it involved a legend about a snapping turtle hitching a ride to the South with a pair of Canada geese. The story was long, however, and I told him it might best be enjoyed another time around the Big Lake Shack fire circle. Mike picked up his turtle shell, turned it over carefully in his hands, and smiled in agreement.

As grandfather and grandson stood beside their truck ready to leave for home, I couldn't help but smile at their appearance. Dick's curly, snow-white hair and beard, his hand clutching his trusty walking stick, the other resting lovingly on his grandson's head. A tired, happy look on his face, with pride exuding from every pore. Mike's boots caked with mud, dry grass and shoestrings trailing behind, pants plastered to his legs, shirt hanging out, one hand grasping his turtle shell, the other round his Grampa's waist, bonded together for all time, his face, turned up toward Grampa's, wearing a smile that said, *I've got the very best grampa in the whole world!*

As they drove away, I reckoned I agree with Mike on that count and that Grampa Dick had a pretty darn good grandson beside him as well.

Cowboy Kenny and the Swamp Steers

The Whitman Swamp is wild and foreboding country. One of the last remnants of seasonally flooded hardwood swamps along the Upper Mississippi River, the area encompasses about six thousand acres. It is a place where wild things thrive and people generally do not.

Over the past forty years, I have, at one time or another, traveled over every square foot of this mysterious, unique place. Four primitive camps are scattered throughout the swamp; half of these are mine. All of them were "grandfathered" in; no more can be built, in accordance with state law.

On one hand, the Whitman Swamp can be gentle and beautiful; on the other, harsh and unforgiving. It naturally follows that I recall a great many good and wonderful experiences from my swampland travels—as well as some happenings that weren't so good, some that were downright awful, and a few that fall into the category of realized nightmare.

Mary Kay and I were taking a late afternoon walk with our dogs, Spider and Webby, in the High Ground Woods near Big Lake Shack. The late April sun brought warmth to the Earth. As our little family of four strolled along the two-wheeled dirt road winding through the woods, we came across freshly emerged stinging nettles, bedstraw, and wild violets. Mary Kay stooped often to touch the green upstarts, to revel in their growth. She is truly a child of the Earth. She loves to dig in the dirt and nurture plants of all kinds, whether wild or domestic.

It made me feel good to see Mary Kay smile, to feel her enthusiasm, and to watch the spring in her step increase. The dogs' steps, while always lively, seemed springier as well. Webby and Spider made frequent side trips to examine bushes, brush piles, and tree stumps. They "read" the signs and scents left by the woods' ever passing parade of birds

Illustration by Tom Kelley, courtesy of the U.S. Fish and Wildlife Service

and critters. Here and there the dogs left their own "calling card," to be deciphered by the next passerby.

At Big Lake Shack, Mary Kay and I walked down to the weathered old boat docks, where we sat on the rough planks and watched the feathered ones frolic on the lake. The dogs forayed along the shores. Blue-winged teal, mallards, wood ducks, and Canada geese noisily proclaimed their delight in the lovely spring evening. Scattered flocks traded back and forth in the air, while males performed water ballets in their finest springtime mating dress for a single female.

We again took up our walking sticks, and the dogs soon joined us. Mary Kay patted the top of Spider's head.

"My God," she exclaimed. "What did that dog roll in this time?"

I took a whiff. "Hooeee, smells like dead fish to me!" A white sticky goo was smeared along the sides of Spider's sleek black neck.

Spider had long ago established a reputation as a genuine connoisseur of stenchy things. She had rolled in everything from fresh hog manure to long-dead turtles. However, well-aged fish seemed to be her all-time favorite. Her nickname, Miss Piggy Pig, was well earned.

Now it was up to the shack for a couple of rags and a bar of soap. When I returned to the lake, Spider wagged her tail and smiled at me as if to say, *I imagine I'm gonna get a bath now, ain't I, Dad?* If there was one thing Spider liked better than rolling in stenchy stuff, it was water of the swimming kind. She swam alongside the dock, where I kneeled down and sudsed her up good and proper. We went back to the bank, where she shook several times. I soaped her up, then sent her back in the water. When she came back, I bent over, drew in a full breath, and declared that little Miss Piggy Pig smelled like a well-bathed dog instead of a sun-ripened fish.

Mary Kay and I exchanged glances as Webster came from his hiding place in the brush. Like any red-blooded boy, he detested baths. Now he knew that the coast was clear.

The four of us tromped up the slope to the shack. The rags were hung to dry, the soap put away for next time. It wasn't a question of *if* we would need them again; it was a question of *when*. Spider would always be Miss Piggy Pig.

We regrouped on the dirt road, which led downhill through a narrow strip of lowland forest bordering the swamp. In my usual slow-moving way, I brought up the rear of our little troupe.

Before long, our case of spring fever returned. The robins sang from the trees. Blackbirds did likewise in the marsh. A pair of wood ducks *eek-eek-eek*ed their way skyward, after we startled them off their preening log in a roadside slough.

We had just passed the slough when Mary Kay pointed near her feet.

"What on Earth are these tracks from?" she asked. By the time I got next to her, she had already figured it out. "Unless a herd of moose has migrated south from Canada to the Mississippi River," she said, "there are some cows on the loose."

"Cows!" I barked. "Cows running around in the swamp!"

The tracks cut a trail ten feet wide in the soft dirt. We followed the unmistakable huge prints back to where they had entered the swamplands: the edge of the work-land fields that rimmed the eastern perimeter of the lowland woods. Yup, they were cows all right. They had come across the open fields from Joe Greshik's farm about a mile to the east.

We turned and followed the tracks back across the dirt road, through the narrow strip of lowland woods, and up to the edge of a small marshy slough. We wore no rubber boots, so we could follow no farther. We stood gawking at the mud-spattered cow trail leading across the slough.

"This cow runaway could prove to be Trouble with a capital T," I said.

Mary Kay heartily agreed.

A few moments later, voices drifted over the slough. Soon, several people approached. "That you, Kenny?" one of them hollered out.

I answered that it was me.

Soon, five people filed across a fallen log bridge over the slough. They were short of breath, wringing wet with sweat, and flushed in the face.

The posse consisted of Joe Greshik Senior, his son Joey, Joey's son Keith, a friend of Keith's, and the Greshik's hired hand, Loyley Seifert.

They told the horror story of how nine mixed-breed steers, weighing about seven to eight hundred pounds, had escaped from the feed lot earlier that day. The five poor souls standing before us had followed the steers into the Whitman Swamp and had been on a cattle chase nonstop ever since. The steers had gone more than half a mile through trees, prickly ash, berry bushes, cattails, and a whole lot of that black, boot-sucking, Mississippi mud. Each time the Greshik gang tried to corner the cattle, the beasts broke to the side and went around the men. Each time, the steers ran faster, got wilder, and went deeper into the swamp.

It was almost dark. The Greshiks looked worn to a frazzle. They were ready to call it a day—one that they would just as soon forget.

Joey asked if I would join the roundup the next morning. I had to tell him that I was to do a number of nature talks around the state the next couple of days; however, I would be back Sunday evening to help. We rationalized that giving the runaway steers time might settle them down some. They might even grow hungry and come out of the swamp by themselves.

Sunday afternoon, Keith and I paddled across Big Lake in my old Queen Mary canoe. The Greshiks had put hay and corn along the dirt road where the cattle had entered the swamp, but they hadn't seen hide nor hair of them. Guess the getting-hungry idea didn't pan out.

This day was a carbon copy of the past few. The sun shone bright in a cloudless sky, with little wind and a temperature in the low fifties. Hundreds of ducks rose into the air around our canoe. Tiny droplets of water fell from their bodies, sparkling as they passed through the rays of sun, dimpling the lake's surface like rain. Keith wondered aloud why the ducks didn't act like this during hunting season. I allowed as how it might be 'cause we ain't trying to kill them today. His teeth showed white in a smile.

On the far side of Big Lake, I guided the canoe into Lone Slough. We paddled past Round Pond, then into Long Lake. All along the way, ducks protested the presence of us rude intruders. We beached the Queen Mary on the west side of Long Lake, pulled her from the water, and tied her to a small soft maple tree.

Keith and I followed a wooded swamp ridge south for half an hour before we came across the tracks of the wayward steers. A while later we followed their trail across Tent Camp Slough, through another wooded ridge, then past the Button Brush Pond.

"Balls of fire, Keith," I said. "They're headed for the Marsh Shack!"

Keith shook his head slowly. "We'll find them all right. It ain't where they're going that bothers me. It's the fact that we got to bring them all the way back out of here—that's the real fly in the ointment."

We moved along at a pretty good clip now. The shadows grew long. We simply had to find those critters before dark. Suddenly we heard a long slow *mooooo* come from the Big Woods country. I suggested that we sneak up on them like we would a deer, on account of if those steers spook now, we might never lay eyes on them again.

We started walking real tippy toed. In a little while, I saw movement ahead. We stopped behind a large swamp white oak and looked long and carefully. There they were, all nine of them, a hundred yards from us. A few of the steers were laying down; the rest huddled in a small group. They switched their tails, chewed their cuds, and wiggled their ears back and forth. They looked about as contented as domestic steers could plumb out in the middle of a Mississippi River backwater swamp. As a matter of fact, they reminded me of a herd of water buffalo whiling away the evening hours. I half expected to see a rice paddy.

Keith and I waited in silence until darkness closed in. Then we made our way back to the canoe as quietly as we could and paddled back to Big Lake Shack. From there, we drove to the Greshik farm. We reported to Joey that we had found the steers and "put them to bed" a short distance from the Marsh Shack, basically smack dab in the middle of the Whitman Swamp.

"Holy mackerel, Martha," Joey sputtered. "Way out there? How we ever going to get them out of there?"

"With a whole lot of luck and a lot more work," I answered. We made plans to meet in Joey's farmyard the next morning at eight o'clock in the morning. He would have all the reinforcements he could muster. I bid the Greshiks good night. Tomorrow the chase would begin in earnest.

The next day's dawn revealed high streaky clouds in the eastern sky. A light southerly breeze blew. The sun had been up awhile when I pulled my old Black Bomber pickup truck to a halt in Greshik's farmyard.

Joey had made good his promise to gather fresh recruits. There were nine men, including myself.

The mood was upbeat and jovial. Barry "Chicken" Auer, a chicken-farming neighbor of the Greshiks, figured that as long as we were all wearing hip boots we wouldn't be needing leather chaps to protect our legs from a long day "in the saddle." Bill Kammueller asked if everybody had their bandanas and lariats handy. We guffawed and chuckled as we "mounted up" in several pickup trucks and "rode out" in a cloud of dust.

We stopped at the dirt road where the cattle had crossed into the swamp. This would be our cutoff point. Here, we strung a couple rolls of wooden-lath snow fencing between the soft maples and river birches. Then we parked a pickup truck crossways on the dirt road, spanning each side of the fencing. Joe Senior and Loyley, the oldest men in the group, stayed to guard the cutoff point.

The rest of the crew drove to Big Lake Shack, where we set off by canoe. Our destination was Wet Foot Point, a mile to the west, where Keith and I had left the steers the night before. The Great Greshik Canoe and Cow Chase had commenced.

At the mouth of Long Lake, we beached and tied the canoes to trees. We continued on foot to the Tent Camp

Slough. Here, an old beaver dam spanned shallow, murky waters, creating a muddy, stick-filled bridge—and a possible route by which to guide the steers back to the Greshik farm.

We paused to discuss strategy at some length. Keith and Johnny Jack Beavers, my foster brother, being the youngest and undoubtedly fleetest of foot, would go find the steers and drive them toward the beaver dam; I would accompany them as a "mellowing agent" and forward scout. Meanwhile, the remaining four men would stay here at the beaver dam to construct the second cutoff point.

As the head-'em-off gang began building a "fence" of sticks and brush, Keith, Johnny Jack, and I set off in the direction of the steers. We traveled past the old Tent Camp site until we came to the south end of the Button Brush Pond.

We could see the cattle from here. They were resting in about the same area as last night. Keith stayed behind as a rear guard, while Johnny Jack and I circled behind the steers. We followed the west side of Schultze's Pond, then waded across a hundred yards of marsh to Wet Foot Point. We eased to within fifty yards of the steers.

The steers that were lying down rose to their feet. Soon the whole herd turned away from us and began to move at a steady pace toward Keith. When they saw him, they turned toward the head-'em-off crew at the beaver dam. The three of us simply followed behind. This was a piece of cake, nothing to it.

After several hundred yards of easy traveling, the steers approached the crew at the beaver dam. The cattle stopped dead in their tracks. Their ears came up; their tails twitched back and forth. They began to mill about nervously. We closed the gap around them, forcing the animals closer to the water. We needed them to cross that beaver dam bridge.

Suddenly, all hell broke loose. Steers ran in every direction. Heavy hooves pounded the earth, mud flew, cattle bellered, water sprayed. Men screamed, hollered, and ran. Some, including myself, fell into that black, boot-sucking, Mississippi mud. There was no rhyme or reason, except that the steers wanted to put as much distance between them and us as possible in a very short time. We wanted just the opposite. The steers won.

While some of us extracted ourselves from our "mudded in" position, others untangled themselves from prickly ash thickets. We regrouped by the beaver dam. There was much huffing and puffing. There were also a number of strong adjectives used to describe the steers, all of which seemed useless as there wasn't a steer within earshot to hear those unkind words. Guess that's called "venting."

A couple of the boys didn't have a speck of mud or a scratch, nor a hair out of place. They looked like they had stepped from the pages of a L.L.Bean catalog for a Sunday-afternoon stroll in the park. The question was raised as to where those fortunate fellas were when the proverbial feces struck the fan.

Just as things were really getting heated, Joey informed us that he had seen a number of steers cross the beaver dam bridge in the midst of the turmoil. The steers—at least some of them—were headed in the right direction. Joey wondered if we could stop our venting long enough to take up the chase while there was still enough daylight to maybe, just maybe, get those steers back to his farmyard before dark.

Some semblance of sanity returned to the roundup crew. We crossed the Tent Camp Slough to a wide wooded ridge. There, we fanned out within sight of each other and headed north. Before long, we found fresh steer tracks on a couple of the main deer trails coursing through the woods.

A quarter mile farther on we spied six big black critters moving ahead of us. All was not lost. A renewed sense of hope surged among us. Now if only Old Joe and Loyley had stayed at their post by the snow-fence barrier over the many long hours, then we stood a chance of getting some of the steers home by nightfall.

We needn't have worried. An hour or so later the six steers gathered in front of the snow fence. And there stood Old Joe and Loyley, the picture of patience. They leaned on the fence. Their bib overalls hung loosely on their tall, lean frames. Their tanned, weathered faces showed no hint of anxiety.

Old Joe lifted his voice just enough to be heard over the rustling trees and the stomping of the steers' hooves in the rich black mud: "Now, boys, I want you all to back off a ways. Give them steers some room. Let 'em travel at their own pace. I don't want to hear any hooting and hollering either." His tone carried a quiet authority born of many years as a first-class cattleman.

We younger folks listened up. We moved back and stood quietly in place. Time seemed suspended. For the first time that day, I became aware of the lovely chorus of bird songs scattered throughout the swamp. A fox squirrel scolded us from high atop its tree limb in a tall swamp white oak. A pair of wood ducks flew low overhead and discussed their next safe landing spot.

Two steers turned from the snow fence and slowly walked toward us. They stopped ten yards away and gazed at us with their large, dark, baleful eyes. Everyone maintained dead silence. Not a movement was made. The steers turned once again, their huge muscles rippling beneath their sleek, black, mud-spattered hide, and they rejoined the others.

Presently, one steer crossed the mucky shallow slough. It reached the far bank, crossed the dirt road between the parked pickups, and stood in the open farm field to look back at the others. This served as an "all clear" signal to the rest. One by one the bedraggled bovines made their way across the slough and into the field, where they joined their leader.

The roundup crew followed suit. I brought up the rear. Old Joe and Loyley still leaned on the makeshift fence barrier. As I passed, they nodded and shot a small grin my way. The old-timers had made all the difference in the world.

"See to it that the boys don't crowd the steers on the way home," Old Joe said. "Just guide them in the general direction and don't make them run if you can help it."

An hour later we closed the gate behind the six steers in the Greshik farmyard. They were well fed and watered. We all breathed a sign of relief.

At the end of the day, Keith, Joey, and I made the long walk back to the south end of Long Lake to retrieve the canoes. We each paddled a canoe back to Big Lake Shack. Plans were made to gather in the farmyard at eight o'clock the following morning. There were still three more steers to bring in.

After Keith and Joey left, I retrieved a pillow from the shack and sat in an old chair by the fire circle overlooking Big Lake. *Oh yeah, oh yeah, what a day!* It felt so good to just sit and not move a muscle. I was afraid to close my eyes, for fear of falling asleep right then and there.

The ducks and geese gabbled and the frogs argued in the swamp. The birds twittered sleepily in the woods. Nighttime drew its curtain of darkness over the land.

The next morning, Webster, Spider, Mary Kay, and I enjoyed our daily "natural moment" together. We stood quietly to listen to the sounds of nature, to smell the fresh air, to feel the early morning sun warm our bones and the gentle springtime breeze drift across our faces. It is always a good way to begin a new day.

Then we said our goodbyes. Mary Kay left for her office

at Alma. The dogs stayed at home. I headed for the Greshik farmyard.

The same crew, minus one man, gathered at the farm. We would follow the same strategy as yesterday.

The crew was subdued as we loaded up the pickups. We were sore and tired and knew, with each passing hour, that the missing steers were growing wilder and tougher to corral. This roundup experience was, in all probability, not going to be a "piece of cake." Little did we know that this piece of cake would prove to be too tough to chew and impossible to swallow.

Old Joe and Loyley stayed by the snow-fence cutoff point, as before. This time, we parked two trucks crossways on the dirt road. The rest of us loaded up in the canoes on Big Lake, and we were off. Day two of the Great Greshik Canoe and Cow Chase had begun.

Once again we paddled to the mouth of Long Lake. We pulled the canoes from the water and tied them to trees. This time we left no one at the beaver-dam bridge. We decided to all spread out to find the missing steers. Within the first hour, we found steer tracks leading along the west side of Schultze's Pond. We followed them south into a long, narrow spit of land that divided two large expanses of open marsh. This spit was studded with a few large silver maples, a number of medium-sized river birch, and a sprinkling of small black willows. Here and there, tufts of sedge grasses sprang up from the rich, soggy earth.

Three men went toward the far south end of the narrow peninsula, which ended in the middle of the two marshes. If there were steers down that way, the men would surely find them. Chicken headed in the other direction. Johnny Jack and I waited where we were. The others would holler when they found the steers, and we would go help them.

A pileated woodpecker flew overhead. Its stop-and-go wing beats caused the big bird to rise and fall in a hip-hop flight. It landed on the side of a river birch. We marveled at the large chips that flew as the bird excavated an oblong hole to find its breakfast of fresh insects.

Someone shouted. We listened closely—another shout. Johnny and I set off in the direction of the voice. A hundred yards later, we stopped short. Chicken stood behind a huge silver maple tree. Thirty feet in front of him stood a seven-hundred-pound steer. It faced him squarely.

"Kenny," Chicken hollered, "this here critter's gone over the edge, I think. It's madder than a wet hen on a pile of broken glass with a egg stuck crosswise!"

I slipped over his way to give him a hand. Johnny stayed put while I made my way closer to Chicken and the seemingly deranged steer. I stopped beside a small tree, about four inches around at the base. The steer's roan hide glistened in the morning sun. Its ears pointed straight out from the sides of its head. Saliva dripped from its mouth. Every inch of the critter's body quivered. Its eyes were wide and wild. This animal's body language told me: *I'm tired of being chased and I'm not moving another inch, so what are you going to do about it?*

Chicken, thinking he might get the steer to move, reached down, picked up a stick, and threw it. He got it to move all right. The stick smacked the steer, and the animal put its head down and charged straight at me.

That critter was as quick and as fast as greased lightning. In a heartbeat, the steer was an arm's length from me. I tried to move behind the little tree. A dull thud sounded as the animal's massive shoulder struck the tree and the left half of my body at the same time.

Everything happened in slow motion. My feet left the ground. I drifted through the air. A jolt ran through me as I landed against a small log. I raised my head in time to see the steer come to a thundering halt twenty yards past me. It turned around to face me and lowered its shaggy head. Steamy breath shot from its nostrils. The wild fire of death shone in its eyes. That beastly bovine was about to finish me off.

A thought flashed through my mind: The "natural moment" this morning with Mary Kay and the dogs might have been our last.

From afar, a robin sang. How fitting for a robin to sing my "death song" here in the swamp that I loved so much.

The hooves pounded. The ground shook. I curled in the fetal position beside the log. The steer passed over me, its rank breath filling my nostrils. I expected to feel its weight upon me; however, I did not. No crunching of bones, no pain, nothing.

Chicken and Johnny Jack began hollering and pounding sticks against trees. In a few seconds, they were by my side. They asked me if I could get up. I said I thought I could, and they helped me to my feet. There was no feeling in my right shoulder and arm. They found a seat for me on a rotten tree stump. There was a whole lot of shaking and shivering and quivering done on my part.

"Great balls of fire, that was a close one!" I said over and over.

"I thought you were a goner," Johnny said.

In a short while, Joey and Keith appeared. We told them the story of the steer attack.

"That's it," Joey said. "The roundup is over. When the chasers become the chasees, it's time to quit. Let's go home!"

There was no argument from me or anyone else. We'd had enough. We rounded up the rest of the men and headed out of the swamp.

While we walked back to the canoes, feeling returned to my shoulder and arm in a big way. My shoulder throbbed and sharp pain shot down my arm and into my hand and fingers.

When we finally reached the Long Lake landing site, I climbed into the bow of my Queen Mary and let Johnny Jack paddle me back to Big Lake Shack. We crawled out of the canoes and tipped them upside down.

At the shack, each member of the bedraggled roundup crew found a seat around the fire circle. We discussed the day's startling events. Joey told me I ought to see a doctor and that his farm insurance would cover the cost. I wiggled my fingers, raised my arm up and down, and said I didn't think that would be necessary 'cause being run over by that confounded steer wasn't a whole lot different than falling out of a tree when I was a kid. Keith thought that there was a difference—I was fifty years older now. A few smiles appeared. Chicken said that he noticed, on the ride back to the shack, that I didn't have a paddle in my hand; he figured old Kenny was getting lazy and weak in his old age. Everyone chuckled.

We concluded that the log I landed against had saved me. When the steer charged the second time, it couldn't lower its head enough to grind me into the ground, and when it jumped over the log, its hooves missed me entirely. I shivered and made a silent vow never to complain again when I stumbled over an old rotten log in the woods.

We talked about the plight of the three steers that remained loose in the depths of the swamp. Would they ever be seen again? What misery they would now endure. Only time would tell of their fate.

As my fellow travelers were leaving, they agreed to call me "Cowboy" Kenny in honor of surviving two close encounters with a mad steer. They all took pleasure in the new nickname. So did I. I was only too happy to laugh, to smell the spring air, to hear the bird songs, to feel the warmth of the sun, and to go home to my beloved Mary Kay and Webster and Spider.

Two weeks later, one steer found its way into a farmyard a mile east of where it had last been seen. The Greshiks returned it to the herd on their farm.

The other two steers were never seen again. It has been almost six years since that fateful day of steer-chasing in the swamp. I have often thought of those steers. They were thrust into a strange environment, yet in only a matter of days there surfaced from deep inside them a recollection of times past—a thousand generations removed. They became distrustful of humans and alert in all their senses. Even though the "amenities" of domestic life were no longer available to them, they came to understand that they could and indeed must survive. The roundup crew represented ancient hunters, predators that had to be avoided and, if worse came to worse, fought to the bitter end. This is what the charging steer did with all the honor and dignity of its ancient ancestors. A lesson was there to be learned.

The lesson is this: No matter how far people remove themselves from their hunter-gatherer ancestors, there still dwells within each of us a primeval urge, a connection to the natural world.

Who among us does not look up when Canada geese fly overhead? Who does not feel a tingle up his spine when the coyote howls its woes?

We garner hope when the robin heralds the coming of a new day. There is restfulness when the whippoorwill tells of approaching darkness. Peace is found at night as the frogs argue around the ponds. We gaze up in the sky, filled with wonder at the moon and the stars. Who does not enjoy the beauty of the wildflowers or the scent of plum blossoms wafting on the springtime breeze? Awe wells up inside us as we watch the eagle soar on the homeless blufftop winds.

These things are as they always were and always shall be, for we are all fellow travelers in the great natural Circle of Life.

Illustration by Bob Hines, courtesy of the U.S. Fish and Wildlife Service

RECIPE

Cowboy Kenny Cookies

1	CUP (2 STICKS) BUTTER	1	TEASPOON BAKING SODA
1½	CUPS PACKED BROWN SUGAR	½	TEASPOON SALT
½	CUP GRANULATED SUGAR	2	CUPS QUICK-COOKING OATMEAL
2	EGGS	2	CUPS (12 OZ.) SEMISWEET CHOCOLATE CHIPS
1½	TEASPOONS VANILLA EXTRACT	1	CUP FLAKED COCONUTS
2	CUPS FLOUR		

Preheat oven to 350°. In a mixing bowl, cream butter and sugars. Add eggs and vanilla; beat until fluffy. Combine flour, baking soda, and salt; beat into creamed mixture. Stir in oatmeal, chocolate chips, and coconut. Drop by the tablespoon onto greased cookie sheets. Bake 10 to 12 minutes or until golden brown. Yield: 4 to 5 dozen cookies.

THE BALLAD OF COWBOY KENNY

To be read while enjoying Cowboy Kenny Cookies

Who says cowboys have to ride the range?
This'n herded dogies in a place that's strange.
Now I'll share the story 'bout this weird event,
how I didn't get broken, just badly bent.

The word went out there were steers on the loose
in the home of the muskrat and the old wild goose,
where there's all kinds of water and boot-suckin' mud.
Land there's scarce, though there ain't no flood.

We went with a vengeance to corral them steers,
most of us young, a few up in years.
The trackin' was easy, the catchin' proved tough.
One steer wouldn't move, it'd plumb had enough.

*Illustration by Bob Savannah, courtesy of the
U.S. Fish and Wildlife Service*

He stood there and quivered and shivered and shook.
Small tree there between us, I hated that look.
Then he came for me, head close to the ground.
I wished for a tree much bigger around.

He came on and hit me, threw me sky high.
I let out a scream—sure I would die.
Came down in the mud against a small log.
The beast stepped across me like I was a frog.

Again he came for just one more try.
His breath was like fire, death in his eye.
My moment was here, my own judgment day.
Somehow he missed me, then went on his way.

They say he's still out there roamin' the swamp,
lookin' for someone his big hoofs can stomp.
The thought of that monster, the fear he instills,
brings tears to my eyes, my blood gets the chills.

They all say there's honor and glory to gain.
Maybe they're right, but my mind thinks of pain.
My friends say they'll track and catch 'im alone.
In that much they're right cause I'll be here at home.

Some say Cowboy Kenny's a bald-faced liar.
Come on now, folks, you think he'd conspire
to tell such a fib? You kin bet your last penny
this poem's the truth from old Cowboy Kenny.

Illustration by Charles Douglas, courtesy of the
Canadian Museum of Nature

The Old Woodstove

Head-high cattails, red dogwood, willows, and a zillion foot-trippin' mounds of swamp mud made up the territory between the Marsh Shack and the Big Drain country. It was wild, tangled, boggy country. Few people ever set foot in that consarned area but me. And I did so only in the winter, when I ran a trap line for mink and the few muskrats found in the potholes that dotted the forlorn landscape like tiny, snow-covered skating rinks.

'Bout halfway across that thousand-acre expanse of foot-travelin' misery stood a small grove of good-sized trees—mostly river birch, green ash, silver maples, and swamp white oaks. I called this place the Oasis Woods because many a time, 'long about noon, I'd find relief from my heavy pack here. After kickin' the snow aside, I'd sit down on a folded burlap sack with my back against a large tree, eat some lunch, stretch my legs out, and relax awhile.

One mild, sunny, January-thaw day, I was resting in the Oasis Woods. I noticed something glinting in the noontime sun, a ways back in the woods. When I was ready to hit the trail, I shouldered my pack, picked up my axe, and headed in the direction of that gleamy, glinty thing. After doing a whole lot of lookin' and searchin', I found absolutely nothing and was just about to give it up, thinkin' my eyes had played tricks on me, when I saw what looked to be a piece of metal stickin' out between several driftwood logs.

When I got there I found, of all things, a wood-burning stove. It was surrounded by a small pile of logs that had been placed there by a long-ago springtime flood. As if this wasn't strange enough, an arm-sized silver maple tree was growing right through the middle of the old stove and sticking up through one of the stovetop lids! Oh, I was puzzled all right. I looked at the surrounding area closer than I had ever done before. The more I looked, the more questions entered my mind. How had that stove gotten where it was today? No flood on this Earth could have moved that heavy stove here. Then who could have put it there? Why and when?

Time was a wastin', so I turned tail and followed my trap line to its end near the Big Drain on Indian Creek. It was after dark when I passed back through the Oasis Woods on my way home to the Marsh Shack. I couldn't help but think of the old woodstove and all my questions about it.

The only clue I found during the rest of the winter was a strange-lookin' hole in a silver maple tree that stood ancient, hollow, and dying near the woodstove. The hole was almost square, sixteen inches in diameter, chest high, and the bark around the edges was completely healed over. Weren't no woodpeckers made that one, nor coons, nor any other critter. No sirree, Bob, humans made that hole, and a mighty long time ago at that.

The whole thing remained a mystery until the following summer when I happened upon an old man in town whose family had owned the land where the woodstove now sat, long before the U.S. Army Corps of Engineers built the lock-and-dam system on the Upper Mississippi River.

The man's name was Albert and he was hoeing his garden, nestled between his little wood-frame house and the Burlington Northern railroad tracks. Albert was in his mid-eighties. His eyesight was failing, and I approached within an arm's length before he recognized me. We chatted about the weather, the garden, and the prices on the fur market before I asked him point-blank whether he knew anything about an old wood-burning stove settin' a ways back in the Whitman Swamp.

His eyes narrowed and wrinkles furrowed his suntanned forehead. "You mean out in that grove a trees that sets between the old Marsh Shack and the Big Drain on Indian Creek?"

Bingo! I'd scored a bull's eye!

"That's exactly where that stove is. Reckon you could fill me in on the woodstove story sometime?"

He allowed as how there was no time like the present, seeing as it was so hot in the sun right then. We retired to a makeshift railroad-tie bench in the shade of the little garden shed, where we whiled away the hot August afternoon hours with Albert mostly talkin' and me mostly listenin'.

Albert recounted back to about 1910 when he, a young boy, joined his grampa and dad on their wintertime wood-makin' forays into the Whitman Swamp. A team of horses pulled them in a wooden wagon box atop a large sleigh. The men rode at least five miles over the frozen backwaters, across the marshes, and around the logs until they came to the grove of trees I called Oasis Woods. This was their main camp. Here is where the stove came into play on those bitterly cold mornings. Albert's father had hauled it out there at the turn of the last century. They'd toss some kindling into the stove, add a corncob soaked in kerosene, pile a little split firewood on top, light the whole shebang, and, presto, they had a roaring hot fire.

"Why a stove?" I asked. "Why not a campfire?"

Albert's eyesight might've been poor, but his mind was as sharp as a freshly ground tack. He explained how the stove used less fuel for the heat you got than a campfire. Also, cookin' was easier on the stove. Not as much danger of a runaway wildfire either. Another thing was drying wet clothes—nothin' to it on the stove, but might burn holes in 'em over a campfire.

He told me how his grampa had found a small oblong hole in a large silver maple tree not far from the stove. He had enlarged it every day over noontime for many years, first with his pocketknife and later with a small hatchet, until the hole was almost square. The final hole was deep enough to act as a cache for his sharpening stones and files, spare scarves, mittens, and splitting wedges, along with a host of other small items the woodcutters might need.

Albert said that with all the traveling back and forth, the one cloud of fear that hung over the woodcutters was the very real danger of breaking through the backwater ice. This would have plunged the sleigh, the woodcutters, and the horses to a frigid death in the waters below. A good many times, Albert walked ahead of the horses to test the thickness of the ice with an ice chisel, thrusting it down as hard as he could every few steps.

Their days were filled with backbreaking work, bitter cold, and the possibility of being cut to the bone by a razor-sharp axe or crosscut saw far away from any doctor. Still, Albert said the little family group found much pleasure in their wood-makin' excursions. Most of it centered around the stove. The taste of a hot bowl of homemade soup or his mother's warmed-up apple pie and freshly baked bread. The winter wind moaning through the naked treetops, dry grasses and reeds rattling like frozen sabers in the nearby marshes, his grampa's and father's laughter as they kidded one another about the long icicles melting into their coffee cups from their frosty mustaches and beards. The smell of the horses tied to a birch tree, stomping their feet, whinnying gently to each other, and waiting to return to work.

Oh, Albert said, and the wood smoke that belched from the four-foot section of pipe that stuck up from the stove to serve as a tiny chimney. On some days, it hurried away with the wind; on others, the smoke hung low to the ground and its pungent odor wafted into every nook and cranny of the little woods.

Albert became quiet. The only sounds were the humming of a fly near my head, the song of a robin in the distance, and a smooth sort of whispering from Albert's brown, calloused hands as they moved slowly back and forth along the handle of his worn garden hoe.

As I reached over, shook his hand, and said, "Thanks, I'll have to be movin' along now," I noticed his eyes were welled up with tears.

I walked away some distance, then turned to look back. There stood Albert in his garden, silhouetted against the faded evening sun, thin and frail, worn, old and rusty, yet dignified and honorable, almost like his old stove setting a ways out there in that Oasis Woods.

May

Trout Fishin' and Morel Pickin'

May brings so many things to do that I don't know which to do first. There are canoes to round up from various ponds, lakes, and sloughs, where they've been cached since last autumn's duck-hunting and trapping expeditions. Firewood to load, haul home, and stack in ranks. Camps to spring "houseclean." Boat and canoe docks to repair as the river's floodwaters recede. Catfishing setlines and other fishing gear to mend and sort. And gardening to do—some has usually been done, but there's still much more.

I enjoy these activities too much to call them "chores." They are simply seasonal tasks I've always had to do as a self-sufficient river rat, and I gain satisfaction from doing them.

However, with each passing day I find it harder to concentrate on the task at hand. By mid-month, one eye is focused on the emerging oak leaves and lilac buds while the other eye is focused on the weather signs. My mind drifts off in search of rippling waters, wooded hillsides, and grassy meadows where the afternoon sun lingers 'til dusk. It is there I will find the trout and the mushrooms. It has been a year and my patience is wearing thin.

Soon the oak leaves are the size of small hog's ears and the lilac bushes sport their first sweet-scented blooms. One evening, it rains a fair amount. The next morning dawns

Illustration by Teeda LoCodo

clear and full of sun. The air is warm all day, almost hot in the direct sunlight. The night promises to be one of those frog-singing, toad-trilling, warm spring nights that fosters the growth of morel mushrooms.

These are the signs I've been waiting for. Tomorrow, everything else goes on the back burner 'cause I'll be trout fishin' and morel pickin'.

Fishing for trout and picking morel mushrooms are two early springtime activities that fit together like a hand in the right-sized glove. Each is a real delight. Combine them and you have what's called pure pleasure. There's only one thing that rivals the fishin' and pickin'—that would be the eatin' part of it all!

I have fished for trout in rivers, ponds, lakes, and cricks throughout the countryside. But I have always found the fishing most pleasurable on the small to midsized cricks that meander through woods and meadows with a lazy, cautious ease. These are the sort of flowing waters that perfectly fit my personality and my fishing style. They also lend themselves well to the picking of morel mushrooms—an added bonus to say the least! I've been pickin' morels since I was knee-high to a grasshopper. Here in the heart of Wisconsin's hill country, cricks flow through narrow valleys shaped by the feet of wooded hills, so trout-rich waters and morel-laden forest floors are not far apart. In a day of fishin' and pickin', my attention alternates between the underwater lairs of trout in the valley's crick and the morel mushrooms found in the nearby hills.

In this part of the country, morel season is short, gen-erally three to four weeks, so if I want a year's supply, it behooves me to strike while the iron is hot. The size of the supply depends on weather conditions and the number of dead or damaged American elm trees in my area.

As for pickin' equipment, there ain't much needed! If I'm pickin' near my truck, I carry a five-gallon pail, a small pocket or belt knife, and a walkin' stick. In the case of a long hike, I bring a large backpack, along with some plastic bread sacks or small cloth bags to keep the morels separated a bit so's they don't get "mooshed" down inside the pack.

For me, it's the looking, the searching for those beautiful little morel morsels, that's the most fun. It's addicting, kind of like prospecting for gold, always looking for the next tree where I might find the morel mother lode. In my mind's eye there is always the sight of a yellowish cream-colored oblong growth protruding four to eight inches above the earth. Its exterior is porous, like a sponge. I'm looking for just one, because if I find one, more will most likely be close by.

The best place to locate a morel is in the vicinity of an elm tree stricken with Dutch elm disease. I say vicinity because I have found morels fifty yards or more from their "parent" tree. Spores are what cause morels to grow; they come from the tree's bark. At times, these spores ride the tail of the wind for quite a distance before "choosing" a place to land.

By far the most productive stage in the decay of the elm is a two- to three-year period from when its bark is just beginning to crack until the bark has completely fallen off. I have filled as many as three five-gallon pails full of morels by a single tree, but this was exceptional. Seldom do I find any morels near a totally "naked" elm. At times, morels grow near elms that have been damaged by lightning strikes or windstorms, when branches have been broken off or bark loosened. I have also found morels near other damaged trees, like cottonwoods and even apple trees. But the vast majority grow close to dying elms.

When mushrooms are found, I pull them from the earth, then cut off the "root" end with a sharp knife or pinch it off between my fingers. This allows me to bag them without getting dirt and grit all over each mushroom. At the nearby crick, I split the morels lengthwise and wash them thoroughly in the water to rid them of little crawly things.

There are a number of ways to preserve the mushrooms that can't be eaten fresh. They can be frozen in water or dry-frozen in plastic bags or containers. My favorite method of preservation is to string them on a cord with a large darning needle and hang the morels in a dry, shady place. Or they can be dried in a dehydrator and stored in sealed glass jars. They can be reconstituted in water when you are ready to use them. If I don't use them all for eating purposes, their nut-brown color and peculiar shapes make for great ornamental hangings in the house, cabin, or on the Christmas tree.

Now the main reason behind the whole process of searching, finding, picking, cleaning, and preserving is to eat the mushrooms, but they aren't all that tasty raw, so there's one more crucial step—cooking! Folks prepare morels in a whole host of different ways: deep fried, roasted, pan fried, and blanched. My personal favorite is to get a large cast-iron skillet full of smoking-hot bacon grease. Dredge the mushrooms in a mixture of cornmeal, salt and pepper, and garlic powder. Drop them into the grease; they should be covered with it. Turn them with a fork until they are brown and crispy on all sides. Take them out of the pan and let them drain well. Eat them piping hot. Jumpin' Jehoshaphat! That's what I call mighty mouthwatering morel morsels!

There's only one way to improve that culinary delight, and that's by having some fresh panfried trout to boot. Which brings us around to the other half of our springtime complementary companions.

To me, trout are the kings and queens of all fishes. If one could call a fish noble, the trout would be that fish—though in truth, when trying to catch these wily, wary denizens of cold, clear waters, I've used many other adjectives to describe them, some of which are unprintable on these pages.

As far as I'm concerned, there is greatness in simplicity. This is especially true when it comes to fishing tackle. My first fishing gear consisted of a small willow tree with a length of black, braided cotton string tied to its thin, whippy tip. A small lead sinker and a fishhook was tied to the free end of the string, and I was all set to go fishing. A tiny twist-cap bottle in my hind pocket holding a couple extra hooks and sinkers served as a tackle box. A somewhat rusty, sometimes sharp jackknife rode in my front pocket. My lures were collected along the crick as they were needed: earthworms from a moist, shady bank; a cricket or a grasshopper in a meadow; big, fat, white grubs under a rotting log; and squiggly red leaf worms from beneath the duff on the nearby forest floor. At times, the trout bait came from the crick itself in the form of small strips of chub meat or minnows, fashioned into just the right shape by my trusty pocketknife.

By not having the convenience of a fishing vest or a tackle box crammed full of ready-made lures and baits, I was forced to find my own naturally grown ones, thus learning not only what the trout liked to eat and when they ate them, but how, when, and where to find the trout's favorite foods. This was a long, sometimes tedious, but always interesting education about the makings of a crick and its surroundings. It got to where the finding of the bait became almost as exciting as the catching of a trout! Once in a while, I'd kick over some wet leaves and see a fat leaf worm squirm. When I'd bend down to pick it up, there was sometimes a plump morel not more than two feet away. I didn't know which treasure to pick first. Usually I went for the worm 'cause it could move faster than the mushroom would.

When a trout was caught, its innards and gills were removed and the fish was washed thoroughly in the crick. Next, an arm's length of thumb-sized tree branches with a fork in one end was cut. This was threaded through the mouth and, presto, I had me a stringer. I carried my catch easily and, when I stopped to fish, I shoved the empty end of the stick into the crick bank with the trout cooling in the fresh, clear water. When the bank was too high and steep, I laid the stringer stick directly in the water, with a rock on top of it so it didn't wash away.

To us locals here in the hill country of Buffalo County, there are no streams or creeks: these are all called cricks. Many of our cricks are in places narrow enough to step across, with undercut banks, riffles, open pools, log holes, and all the other kinds of trout lairs in natural abundance.

Two species of trout are found in our cricks: German browns, which were introduced or, as we say, "planted" here many years ago, and brook trout, the native fish to our cricks.

The German brown is generally a secretive, sulky, temperamental fish when it comes to feeding, although when they're in the right mood, they will attack their prey with the reckless abandon of a barracuda. When I'm looking to catch a really big, old-timer brown trout, I head downstream to the tail end of the crick, where the water runs slow and deep. Usually this spot has plenty of minnows, chubs, and frogs for an old square-tailed, hook-jawed lunker to scarf up at its leisure. The best part about end-of-the-crick-fishing is that there ain't many folks who fish here. It just doesn't appear "trouty lookin'" to most anglers, and for the most part, they're right. There aren't a lot of trout, but what's here are bullish brutes that take a good dose of patience and luck to land.

My method of fishing for the big brown trout is simple. I catch a chub, which is an overgrown minnow about three to six inches long. Then I cut one whole side off, leaving the tail attached, bury my fishhook in the end opposite the tail, and sink the "chub fillet" to the bottom of the deepest log-infested hole I can find. Now it's a waiting game.

I'm always surprised at how much there is to do while I'm sitting there doing nothing! This is when I've seen the white-tailed doe and her fawns come to drink from the cool, clear waters. A muskrat swims past my fishing line and crawls on the bank to feed in the lush green grass at my feet. A red-tailed hawk soars across the rosy hue of the setting sun while a killdeer herky-jerkies its way along a sand spit. Want watchable wildlife? Go soak some bait in quiet, deep waters at dawn or dusk and soak up the sights and sounds of the wild things. There is no finer way to enjoy a couple of quiet hours.

With the strike of the trout, the battle is on. Sometimes I catch the fish; sometimes I lose it. No matter, 'cause I'm always the winner when I "tail end" a crick for trout.

My all-time favorite fish among fishes is the native brook trout, perhaps because the first "eatin' size" fish I ever caught was just such a specimen.

I was going into my seventh summer. I had drifted a large leaf worm beneath the long grass, which hung in the water from an undercut bank, when I felt a sharp tap on the fishing line. My willow pole dipped sharply toward the water, tip bent in an arc, and I heaved up. A flopping foot-long trout landed on the grassy bank. I pounced on that poor fish like a fox on a mouse and gripped it tightly in my scrawny little hand. The fish was already off the hook, but I had no intention of returning it to the crick. For the longest time, I knelt there in the meadow staring at my prize, devouring every detail of its sleek body. Brilliant dapples of crimson and yellow were speckled against a pea-green, wormlike background that faded to a creamy white belly with a couple pairs of protruding snow-white tipped fins. There was a slightly upturned hook on the front of the lower jaw and a square tail on the fish's other end.

"A trout!" I repeated over and over. "I've caught a trout!"

At last I took the tightly clutched fish to the edge of the crick and cleaned it with my jackknife. As I washed out its body cavity, the fish's fiery red flesh shone in the bright May sunshine like a precious ruby.

A willow branch stringer was cut, my trophy strung upon it, the willow fishing pole retrieved from the meadow grass, and I headed for home at a quick pace. Every three or four steps, I'd look down to be sure that my beautiful foot-long brook trout was still there.

As the springs and summers of my life came and went, I learned a great deal more about the ways of the native brook trout. A lifelong love affair developed between us.

When fishing for brook trout, I use a combination of hunting and fishing skills. These fish must be stalked.

They live in small cricks—the name "brook" trout is no accident—where there is a much smaller margin for error than in a larger, deeper run. My shadow must never cross the water, nor do these skittish little beauties tolerate heavy footfalls.

As with all trout, I fish for brookies upstream 'cause they face the current in order to capture their food as it drifts down the crick. If a trout sees me, it won't bite. Coming from behind reduces that chance, although there have been times I'd have sworn those little buggers have eyes in the backs of their heads! If the stalking is done well, the biting comes easier, because the brookie is not nearly as finicky as the German brown. No sign of predator trouble and, wham, the brook trout slams the bait with gusto, while the brown trout might be in one of its moods and nothing will get it to bite.

Another reason I love the brookie is the sense of adventure and excitement that derives from following the crick, always moving from deep, dark, shadowy log holes to green, grass-covered undercut banks and swift, gurgling riffles. With each step comes new landscape and discoveries: A patch of spongy-looking morels scattered around an elm tree. A sparrow's nest nestled in a small willow tree. The song of the lark in a nearby meadow. Momma killdeer's broken-wing act across a stretch of sandy cow pasture. On rare occasions, a spotted fawn found hidden in the tall grasses; it moves nothing, not even its eyes, as I pass without stopping to stare. A baby muskrat, its hind feet visible in the crystal water, kicking and paddling frantically while its tiny tail steers toward home in a secret crick-bank den. Now and then a leopard frog leaps for safety, landing with a dull *kaplunk*, like a child tossing a pebble into the water.

Around every bend and curve, in each nook and cranny, beyond the next grove of trees, new expectations are met. Both in and out of the crick, fresh experiences are plentiful while the birds and the wind and the water sing their song of spring.

By the time the shadows have grown long, I have "collected" some of each of the treasure sought: fresh, native trout and bags full of morel mushrooms. Beneath a giant cottonwood, beside a quiet pool, I clean and soak and admire my day's bounty. The gentle movement of the clear water across the snow-white insides of split morels and the brilliant multicolored brookies remind me once again of the shimmering beauty of precious gems. And they are exactly that to me. I gather them and think pleasurably of wood smoke, a cast-iron skillet, savory sizzling brook trout, and fresh, golden brown morel mushrooms.

The robin and the whippoorwill herald the falling of dusk. As I start my homeward journey from this lovely, lonesome, hill-country valley, I am filled with the joys and wonders of Nature, as I have always been. Although I now wear rubber boots and fish with a store-bought fly rod, little else has changed over the past fifty years as to my relationship within the natural Circle of Life. If it has, it's been for the better. My heart is glad.

I guess inside I'm still that little urchin of a ragtag boy, pant legs rolled up above suntanned feet, walking along a meandering crick with my thin, whippy, willow fishing pole slung over my shoulder. Happy and carefree as the springtime breezes that taunt and tease the newborn leaves into singing a lullaby.